Praise for
GODLY AMBITION

"*Godly Ambition* is a vital guide for a culture where people are desperate to discover their authentic self. Ruslan KD helps us strengthen our identity in Christ, address our wounds, and cultivate habits aligned with God's purpose. His practical and biblical insights on navigating setbacks and removing distractions will give hope and help to many."

—JOSHUA BROOME, speaker, author, and pastor

"Ambition can be a dangerous thing that shrivels our souls, and Christians sometimes avoid it. But in this inspiring book, Ruslan KD helps us understand that there is a *Godly* ambition, one that is often sorely lacking in the church. Sharing honestly from his own experiences, he shows us how to cultivate the right kind of ambition, then gives practical suggestions for how to achieve it. Do you long for your life to count? Do you want to give yourself to a noble cause? Read this book and let it guide you."

—GAVIN ORTLUND, pastor, professor, and author of
Why God Makes Sense in a World That Doesn't

"*Godly Ambition* is a road map for anyone trying to navigate the tension between career and calling, hustle and holiness. Ruslan KD doesn't just inspire—he equips you with practical steps and biblical wisdom to pursue big goals without losing your soul. If you've ever wrestled with starting, quitting, or wondering what's next, this book will meet you right where you are."

—JON ACUFF, *New York Times* bestselling author of
Soundtracks: The Surprising Solution to Overthinking

"In *Godly Ambition*, Ruslan KD speaks to the tension within every visionary. This book is a clarion call back to kingdom-centered purpose and faithfulness, which is anchored in our identity in Christ. Every follower of Jesus needs to read this book and embrace its message."

—BENNY PEREZ, speaker, author, coach, and lead pastor of ChurchLV

"Ruslan KD cuts through the noise with a message Christians desperately need: Your ambition can be holy. *Godly Ambition* doesn't waste time with vague spiritual platitudes or hustle culture hype; instead, it delivers a battle-tested framework for channeling your drive in ways that glorify God. This is the rare book that will both fire you up and ground you, challenging you to steward your talents while keeping Christ at the center."

—MIKE SIGNORELLI, lead pastor of V1 Church

"*Godly Ambition* is a wake-up call for the church today, a wake-up call for Christians to use their gifts for the kingdom rather than personal gain, and a wake-up call to define success biblically rather than by the metrics of the world. And yet this book is also practical. With transparency and wisdom, Ruslan KD offers readers a game plan for lasting impact. I loved this book and am confident you will too."

—SEAN McDOWELL, PhD, is a YouTuber, author, and professor of apologetics at Talbot School of Theology

"In *Godly Ambition*, Ruslan KD offers more than insight—he offers his story, forged through pain and redeemed by purpose. This is not just a book of wisdom; it's a testimony of how God never wastes our pain. From brokenness to bold conviction, he shows how surrendering our wounds to Christ can birth a calling greater than we imagined. His transparency, humility, and practical wisdom challenge believers to live with intentionality, integrity, and faith. *Godly Ambition* is a road map for stewarding our time, talent, and treasure for eternal impact—without losing our soul in the process. I wholeheartedly recommend this book to anyone ready to pursue their God-given calling with courage and clarity."

—JEFF BRADFORD, president of Human Coalition

"*Godly Ambition* is a wake-up call for anyone who senses there's more to life than surviving and scrolling. Ruslan KD combines timeless wisdom with real-world grit to challenge you toward purpose, perseverance, and Christ-centered impact. This isn't just a book—it's a blueprint for becoming the person God designed you to be."

—ANDREW F. CARTER, husband, dad, pastor, and author

"In a time when ambition is either idolized or vilified, *Godly Ambition* offers a much-needed recalibration. As a semi-professional artist with creative pursuits outside of YouTube and the wife of a part-time hot air balloon pilot, I appreciate the beauty of bold, disciplined, and unique goals. Ruslan KD's message is a refreshing reminder that when ambition is surrendered to Christ, it becomes a gift to steward, not suppress. It becomes *Godly* ambition. Through his own story, professional transparency, and biblical insight, he challenges readers to reject apathy and self-centered hustle and instead pursue a disciplined life fully surrendered to Christ. *Godly Ambition* is practical, biblical, and inspiring, showing that hard work, big dreams, and deep faith are partners in God's kingdom work."

—MELISSA DOUGHERTY, Christian apologist and author of *Happy Lies*

"Talents are meant to be used in Christ's service—in both the ambition we're called to and its godly stewarding. Ruslan KD takes this seriously. As a brother walking this path, he has invaluable, heartfelt, and hard-won wisdom to share. Lean in. This book will do you much good."

—GLEN SCRIVENER, director of Speak Life, author of *The Air We Breathe,* and presenter of online evangelism course 321

"*Godly Ambition* is a must-read for every Christian who wants to dream big while still honoring God. I wish I'd had this book when working out my calling in life. It would've saved me years of frustration."

—ZACH WINDAHL, author and content creator

"Ruslan KD's book confronts one of the most ignored dangers of our day: the idolization of ambition. Ambition, though a good thing, is often exploited for selfish reasons rather than submitted to Jesus. This book is a timely guide for anyone seeking to steward their gifts for God's glory without falling into the traps of hustle culture or passivity. This is a must-read for anyone wanting to live out their calling with faith and integrity."

—KB, rapper and author of *Dangerous Jesus*

"Ruslan KD's honesty, truthfulness, and authenticity are on full display in this book. He speaks poignantly about *why* God has put us on this earth and *what* we're called to do. The gospel is not a vitamin you can 'try'—it's a historically grounded, heart-changing, truth-gripping reality. Ruslan KD shows how we can live with passion, prayer, and practicality. After you read this book, read it again—there's so much wisdom here you don't want to miss."

—WES HUFF, apologist and YouTuber

GODLY AMBITION

GODLY AMBITION

UNLOCKING THE
FULL POTENTIAL OF
YOUR TIME, TALENT,
AND TREASURE

RUSLAN KD

FOREWORD BY
JONATHAN "JP" POKLUDA

WATERBROOK

WaterBrook

An imprint of the Penguin Random House Christian Publishing Group,
a division of Penguin Random House LLC

1745 Broadway, New York, NY 10019

waterbrookmultnomah.com
penguinrandomhouse.com

All Scripture quotations, unless otherwise indicated, are taken from the Holy Bible, New International Version®, NIV®. Copyright © 1973, 1978, 1984, 2011 by Biblica Inc.™ Used by permission of Zondervan. All rights reserved worldwide. (www.zondervan.com). The "NIV" and "New International Version" are trademarks registered in the United States Patent and Trademark Office by Biblica Inc.™ Scripture quotations marked (ESV) are taken from the ESV® Bible (The Holy Bible, English Standard Version®), copyright © 2001 by Crossway, a publishing ministry of Good News Publishers. Used by permission. All rights reserved. Scripture quotations marked (KJV) are taken from the King James Version. Scripture quotations marked (NLT) are taken from the *Holy Bible*, New Living Translation, copyright © 1996, 2004, 2015 by Tyndale House Foundation. Used by permission of Tyndale House Publishers, Carol Stream, Illinois 60188. All rights reserved.

Copyright © 2025 by Kings Dream Entertainment
Foreword by JP Pokluda copyright © 2025 by Penguin Random House LLC

Penguin Random House values and supports copyright. Copyright fuels creativity, encourages diverse voices, promotes free speech, and creates a vibrant culture. Thank you for buying an authorized edition of this book and for complying with copyright laws by not reproducing, scanning, or distributing any part of it in any form without permission. You are supporting writers and allowing Penguin Random House to continue to publish books for every reader. Please note that no part of this book may be used or reproduced in any manner for the purpose of training artificial intelligence technologies or systems.

WATERBROOK and colophon are registered trademarks of Penguin Random House LLC.

Grateful acknowledgment is made to Avery, an imprint of Penguin Publishing Group, a division of Penguin Random House LLC and Random House Business, an imprint of The Random House Group Limited, London, for permission to reprint "Figure 3: Three Layers of Behavior Change" from *Atomic Habits: An Easy & Proven Way to Build Good Habits & Break Bad Ones* by James Clear, copyright © 2018 by James Clear. Used by permission of Avery, an imprint of Penguin Publishing Group, a division of Penguin Random House LLC and Random House Business, an imprint of The Random House Group Limited, London. All rights reserved.

Library of Congress Cataloging-in-Publication Data

Names: KD, Ruslan author
Title: Godly ambition : unlocking the full potential of your time, talent, and treasure / Ruslan KD.
Description: First edition. | Colorado Springs : WaterBrook, [2025] |
Includes bibliographical references.
Identifiers: LCCN 2024060715 | ISBN 9780593602461 hardcover | ISBN 9780593602478 ebook
Subjects: LCSH: Ambition | Success--Religious aspects--Christianity
Classification: LCC BJ1533.A4 K3 2025 | DDC 179/.9--dc23/eng/20250616
LC record available at https://lccn.loc.gov/2024060715

Printed in the United States of America on acid-free paper

1st Printing

First Edition

The authorized representative in the EU for product safety and compliance is
Penguin Random House Ireland, Morrison Chambers, 32 Nassau Street, Dublin D02 YH68, Ireland.
https://eu-contact.penguin.ie

BOOK TEAM: Production editor: Jessica Choi • Managing editor: Julia Wallace
• Production manager: Kevin Garcia • Copy editor: Tracey Moore
• Proofreaders: Karissa Silvers, Marissa Earl

For details on special quantity discounts for bulk purchases, contact
specialmarketscms@penguinrandomhouse.com.

Foreword

I have wrestled with ambition my whole life. Maybe you have too.

How much do I strive? How much do I surrender? Do I hustle, or do I "let go and let God," as the framed Hobby Lobby art above my parents' toilet read?

These questions aren't just theoretical for me—they have shaped my journey, especially in ministry. On one hand, I want to give everything I have to God's work. I want to maximize my gifts, my time, my impact. On the other hand, I know striving apart from God's power is not just exhausting—it's dangerous. It leads to pride, burnout, and an identity tangled in what I do instead of who I am in Christ.

That's why this book matters.

I met Ruslan because we did a podcast together. I drove to the middle of a neighborhood, pulled up to an unassuming house, and waited for him to appear. When he came out, we didn't walk through the front door. Instead, we went around back to his studio—a creative command center where he "cooks," as the cool kids say.

What I saw there left an impression on me.

Ruslan is a worker. Not just any worker. A relentless, strategic, thoughtful worker. He has a team helping him produce a video podcast that would make any major news network jealous. He understands algorithms, live editing, and digital engagement at a genius level. But underneath all that, there's something even more important: a man who loves God and his Word, and cares deeply about reaching people with the truth.

Ruslan's work ethic isn't about chasing fame or clout. It's about something much deeper. It's about why he works in the first place.

That's a question all of us have to ask ourselves—what's our *why*?

What's driving us? Is it success? Status? Influence? If our ambition is fueled by a need to prove ourselves or build our own kingdom, it will eventually leave us empty. But when our *why* is anchored in something greater—when our motive is to glorify God and steward what he's entrusted to us—our ambition has eternal significance.

Ruslan understands this at a deep level. He doesn't just create content for clicks; he creates with conviction. He doesn't just chase trends; he discerns the times. I observed this firsthand as we recorded the podcast and then drove around together afterward. I was struck by how well connected and well informed he is—not just in digital media but in the subculture of hip-hop. He's an expert. He knows the history, the artists, the movements shaping culture today. He understands the beats that people move to and the deeper narratives shaping their worldview.

And yet, he isn't just immersed in culture—he's engaging it. Speaking into it. Calling people toward something higher.

I think about 1 Thessalonians 4:11: "Make it your ambition

to lead a quiet life: You should mind your own business and work with your hands, just as we told you."

This is one of those verses we don't talk about enough. We live in a world that celebrates hustle culture, yet Scripture calls us to a different kind of ambition—one marked by diligence, wisdom, and a life so faithful that it speaks for itself.

This book makes that come alive.

Ruslan has put words to a tension we all feel but often struggle to resolve. He shows that godly ambition isn't about chasing success at the expense of our souls, nor is it about passively waiting for God to do all the work. It's about walking the narrow path between faith and action, dependence and diligence, humility and hunger.

You hold in your hands a guide for that journey.

As you read these pages, I pray that you find clarity and conviction about what it means to work hard for the right reasons. That you'll step into your calling with purpose, not pressure. That you'll learn to strive in a way that honors God—where your ambition isn't about building your kingdom, but his.

And when you're finished, I hope you won't just think differently. I hope you'll live differently. Because godly ambition doesn't just shape careers. It shapes legacies.

—JP Pokluda
Lead pastor of Harris Creek Baptist Church,
bestselling author, and host of the
Becoming Something podcast

Contents

Foreword . . . . *v*

Introduction . . . . *xi*

PART 1: *Clarify Your Vision*

1. *Is Ambition Bad or Good?* 3
2. *Identity: Know Who You Are* 25
3. *Calling: Know Why You're Here* . . . 41

PART 2: *Cultivate Your Growth*

4. *Master the Fundamentals* 63
5. *Stack Your Talents* 75
6. *Follow the Favor* 85
7. *Defeat Distraction* 95
8. *Collaborate with Others* 111
9. *Connect to Community* 125
10. *Pray Boldly* 147
11. *Prepare for Setbacks* 163

Conclusion 177

Acknowledgments 191

Notes 193

Introduction

"It was the best of times, it was the worst of times," Charles Dickens wrote in A Tale of Two Cities. "It was the season of light, it was the season of darkness, it was the spring of hope, it was the winter of despair."[1] If this doesn't capture the era we currently live in, I'm not sure what does.

On one hand, the modern age is filled with opportunity. Things are looking up. Consider that your smartphone has "more computing power than all the greatest supercomputers through the turn of the 21st century."[2] With a few taps of your finger, you can have anything delivered to your doorstep, including lunch, a pair of jeans, new kicks—even a car! Ancient kings and queens would marvel at the tools at our disposal.

Education is also on the rise. "In 2021, about 37.7 percent of the U.S. population who were aged 25 and above had graduated from college or another higher education institution"—a significant increase from 7.7 percent in 1960.[3]

And we enjoy more entertainment and leisure than previous generations. According to one report, as of 2023, there were 2,286 streaming services in the United States.[4] No matter where you are, you can stream your favorite show or choose from one of the six million podcast titles or one hundred million songs on Spotify.[5]

On the other hand, in Dickens's words, we're also living in "the season of darkness" and "the winter of despair." It feels like things are going down. Despite the amenities of modern life, deaths of despair—referring to deaths from "suicide, opioid overdoses and alcohol-related illnesses"—are on the rise.[6] For as much as smartphones and social media promise to "connect" us to others, they've created an unprecedented epidemic of anxiety, depression, and loneliness.

Economically, many of us are struggling. The average person today is living paycheck to paycheck. According to Bankrate, more than one in three (36 percent) of U.S. adults had more credit card debt than money saved in an emergency savings account, and 56 percent of U.S. adults would opt to borrow money rather than "pay for an emergency expense of $1,000 or more . . . from their savings account."[7]

Health trends are equally concerning. About 73 percent of Americans are overweight, with 42 percent of those classified as obese.[8]

It's a strange paradox, isn't it? Somehow the efficiencies of technology, which promise to make our lives easier, have left us more exhausted. Our obsession with productivity has left us feeling hopelessly behind. We should be sailing across a pleasant sea of entertaining thrills, but instead we're drowning in a bottomless abyss of content.

It's the best of times and the worst of times.

FRUSTRATED AMBITION

Do you ever feel like life has stacked the deck against you, but you can't quite figure out why? You have dreams, goals, and ambitions. Yet while you *thought* you were running toward them, it's like someone secretly plopped you onto a treadmill, and you're starting to wonder whether you're running in place, no closer to your destination than when you started.

As if this weren't overwhelming enough, add to the mix the endless opportunities to compare ourselves to others, all of whom seem to be further along, more successful, and effortlessly gliding toward their goals. Of course, this is an illusion, but it nonetheless solidifies our sense of aimlessness and drains us of ambition.

As a content creator, I've spent thousands of hours talking with people, and I've come to believe that while all of us long to fulfill our callings, most of us aren't sure where to start. You have gifts to offer the world, but they lie dormant because you're just trying to keep your head above water. You know God's placed you on this planet for a reason, but distraction and discouragement feel like a wet blanket that's smothering your dreams. Maybe you've put in serious effort toward a goal, only to have it crash and burn. Now you'd rather play it safe than fail again. I've been there too.

MY STORY

By all accounts, the fact that I now run a seven-figure media business is a miracle. As a refugee kid who was raised by a single mom battling alcoholism and whose dad was barely around, life didn't set me up on the fast track to success. I was born in

Baku, Azerbaijan, but due to hostility toward Armenians in my home country in the 1980s and '90s, our family fled to America. We arrived in California in 1991 with hopes for a fresh start, and while there was plenty of opportunity, my childhood was fraught with dysfunction.

One day, I found a letter with lipstick marks all over it and assumed it was a love note from my mom to my dad. It wasn't. I delivered the letter to Dad, not knowing Mom had written it for her boyfriend back in Baku. This discovery pushed my parents' already teetering marriage over the edge. My dad moved out, and internally, I felt responsible.

My mom, who was unexpectedly single in a new country and had no marketable skills, did the best she could. It would take her five years to find employment, so in the meantime, we lived on welfare, which in those days was $650 a month. Of that, $450 went straight to rent, which left $200 for us to live on.

Besides our economic struggles, Mom also had questionable taste in men. She cycled through boyfriends, most of them violent, until things escalated one night when one of them smashed a drinking glass into her face. Later, that same boyfriend laughed when he told me, "One day you're going to wake up and I'm going to kill your mom." Thankfully, she ended that relationship.

My dad visited me often after he first moved out, but at a certain point, he got in a fight with one of my mom's new boyfriends. She jumped into the scuffle, slashing my dad's face with her high heel. As the cops arrived, she told me to lie and say she didn't do it. After that, Dad visited only once a year. Eventually, he remarried and had a whole new family to care for. The irony is, he lived two streets down from me. He was close in proximity, but he might as well have lived across the world.

I won't rehash the stats about how fatherlessness impacts a young man's likelihood of success, but it's not surprising that in fifth grade I was arrested for breaking into a neighbor's house.

Then there was the time in eighth grade when my mom never came to pick me up from basketball practice. Turns out, she'd gotten a DUI on the way to school and had to spend the night in jail, so I scrambled to find a way home. I don't say this to shame my mom, whom I love dearly. (In recent years, God has deepened and enriched our relationship, which I'm so thankful for.) I don't even see myself as a victim. Because as difficult as my growing-up years were, I've experienced the radical transformation of Jesus and, despite the odds, have done quite well for my family.

I tell you all this because if I can do it, *you can too.*

I truly believe that. My circumstances didn't define me, because God had greater plans for my life. So whatever is holding you back, discouraging your heart, or whispering "You'll never make it" is no match for the will of God. Everything I share in this book is meant to stoke the fire of your ambition—to remind you that no matter where you come from, you're capable of leaving a mark on this world.

If God is for you, who can be against you (Romans 8:31)?

That said, the journey is hard because the world is broken. Even as God's Spirit puts wind in your sails, the enemy stirs up stormy seas to intimidate you. Let's get you ready for those moments so you can become the person you were born to be.

WHAT THIS BOOK IS ABOUT

In this book, I'll share some of my greatest learnings, which have helped me love Jesus more, become a better father and husband, launch a record label, tour as a Christian rapper, and create a thriving YouTube channel. If your vocational interests are different from mine (let's say, for instance, you're an accountant, teacher, lawyer, chef, or stay-at-home parent), these principles will still be immensely helpful to you. I'm writing to those hungry to clarify their calling—people who want to use the time, talent, and treasure God has given them to bless others and build the kingdom.

This book is wildly practical, meant to help you chase the dreams God has put on your heart—in the *real world,* not a fantasy. I know you have responsibilities pressing on you, so I keep my advice actionable and short.

At the same time, this book is spiritual—it goes beyond self-help or life hacks to speak to God's vision for your life. Too often, Christians pay lip service to faith, but it has little bearing on their ambition. In these pages, God is not a placeholder so we can get to the "real stuff." He's the center of my message. I want to show you how the spiritual and practical intertwine. God invites you to partner with him as you discover and live out your calling.

THE JOURNEY AHEAD

In part 1, we'll define what godly ambition is and show how it's the fuel for everything you do. These first three chapters lay a crucial foundation, answering questions like these:

- Is ambition a good thing or not? And how do you know? (chapter 1)
- What does it mean to find your identity in Christ, and why does it matter? (chapter 2)
- How do you discover your calling? (chapter 3)

In part 2, I'll unpack the most valuable lessons I've learned while following Jesus, loving my family, and building profitable businesses. This is where you'll glean strategies, including these:

- How to maximize your current situation while dreaming about the future (chapter 4)
- How to cultivate a marketable, one-of-a-kind skill set (chapter 5)
- How to follow God's lead when he takes you in unexpected directions (chapter 6)
- How to defeat distraction and achieve your goals (chapter 7)
- How to collaborate effectively with others (chapter 8)
- Why your church community is essential to your ambition (chapter 9)
- How to make prayer a central part of your life (chapter 10)
- How to navigate unforeseen setbacks and build resilience (chapter 11)

I hope these outcomes excite you. If you had told six-year-old me I'd be writing a book about how to "make it" in life, I would have laughed. I was the kid who struggled to read. The student whom teachers never expected much from. The guy statistically slated for trouble. Praise be to God that he had other plans!

If you follow the guidance laid out in this book, don't expect everything in your life to instantly improve. Progress can be slow. Nor am I implying that we should pursue God merely to gain from him. At times, following Jesus leads to *more* challenges and suffering, depending on your circumstances and context.

The goal is not to get rich or become famous but to maximize the gifts, talents, and opportunities God has given you. The goal is to identify your next step. To pray and strategize about what he's calling you to do with the resources in your hands. The goal is to get you unstuck, dreaming again, fired up.

I want you to discover the abundant life Jesus promises (John 10:10). As a child of God, you are created to do great things. You are not average, my friend. You are not called to settle.

You are made for godly ambition.

PART 1

Clarify Your Vision

1

Is Ambition Bad or Good?

"Can I talk to you for a second?"

I had just finished speaking at a young adults ministry, when a young man approached me. He was sharply dressed, was earnest, and looked perplexed.

He explained he was a visual artist. Curious, I took a moment to check out his work online—it was genuinely impressive.

"This is great stuff. I definitely think you have something special here. Are you pursuing art full-time?"

"No, I'm working twenty hours a week. Other than that, just kicking it."

I took a beat. "Gotcha. Well, do you *want* to pursue your art full-time?"

"I'm not sure. I don't want to become too successful, ya know?"

As I looked at this young man, taking his first steps as a gifted artist, I understood the tension he felt. As a "Christian influencer" (a title I'm not particularly fond of, by the way), I've thought *a lot* about how to wield influence as a follower of Jesus. Most days, at least one stranger recognizes me from my YouTube channel. That might sound exciting—and to be sure there are rewarding moments—but it's also dangerous. If I'm honest, there's a broken part of me that *wants* recognition to feel worthwhile. Validation is a drug. One hit is never enough, and before long, you need more and more to feel whole.

Perhaps you wonder something like this:

> *Is it wrong to want success?*
> *How do I find my calling in life?*
> *How do I start or run a business with integrity?*
> *How do I keep success from corrupting me?*
> *How do I make the most out of my life and honor God?*

If you've wrestled with any of these questions, this book is for you. In the church, *ambition* sometimes feels like a dirty word. We're ashamed to admit we want things—that we're driven to create, build, and achieve. In some circles, it's fashionable to depend on God but "worldly" to hustle.

That said, this young man's response saddened me. He was *full* of potential but held back, fearing that success would corrupt his character. It's the equivalent of avoiding the gym because you don't want to get too jacked. Instead, why not hit the gym and see what happens? Chances are, you'll live a happier and healthier life.

The same principle applies to your gifts: Why not try to maximize your impact? While it's noble to prioritize character, before you worry about the trappings of success, let's get financially stable. Let's build a network of support and collaboration. Let's start a movement. Let's make some noise about what you're up to.

If you stop before you start, in this volatile economy, with all the distractions around you, you've already lost. Too much ambition can be a problem, but just as often I see people with *no* ambition. Apathy is a silent dream killer, and it's taking way too many people down.

I'm here with good news: There *is* a way to pursue excellence—even success—without losing your soul. There *is* a way to dedicate your drive to God. To be sure, chasing ambition like Jesus does looks *very* different from chasing success like the world does. You will have to unlearn some things culture has hammered into you.

In fact, you've likely heard two lies about ambition, and they're possibly influencing you in negative ways—holding you back from the type of ambition God wants for you. Let's look at these lies now.

LIE 1: ALL AMBITION IS EVIL

In the church, many view ambition as a vice more than a virtue. It's tacky, like that Christmas sweater you pull out once a year. It fits awkwardly and makes you feel out of place. Some of my friends who are lead pastors express mixed feelings about ambition. On one hand, they deeply desire for their congregation members to be ambitious in the sense of striving toward the fullness of what God has for them—pursuing godly lives and maximizing their God-given potential. However, they also caution against the darker side of ambition, which can emerge even within church walls. This manifests when individuals start seeking additional authority and power prematurely, often without demonstrating the humility to submit to church leadership. The tension of godly versus prideful ambition illustrates why this can be such a polarizing topic in a church setting; it has the potential to either foster growth and spiritual maturity or lead to discord and power struggles.

Living in a culture that flippantly uses the word *blessing* to celebrate material success makes this topic even more complicated, as if God were a genie who exists only to grant our wishes. I don't want to spend my life taking from my Father's hand while missing his heart.

We plaster over our apathy with platitudes about staying humble. In reality, though, we're playing it safe. Or settling for less than our God-given potential.

Cue the stereotypical thirty-year-old living in his grandmother's basement. Or the person who stays in a dead-end job for decades because she's too comfortable where she is and too afraid to take a new risk. God doesn't call us to sail ahead recklessly, but he often calls us out of the boat. Some of us are a little too comfy sitting at the oars, drifting aimlessly.

Yet when we look at Jesus's teachings, we see that he doesn't rebuke our desire for greatness. He doesn't dismiss ambition or tell his disciples to settle down and chill. If anything, he stirs up *more* ambition in their hearts. He radically redefines what it means to be great.

More on that in a moment, but first, let's expose another aspect of this first lie: Some say ambition is narcissistic. A few years ago, an up-and-coming pastor started making waves online. In a sermon clip that went viral, he declared that all ambition is evil—even calling it "demonic." He referenced James 3:14, which states, "If you harbor bitter envy and selfish ambition in your hearts, do not boast about it or deny the truth." As I watched, the irony was impossible to ignore: a sharply dressed pastor, standing on a professionally lit stage with top-notch audio quality, preaching against ambition. Really? Why else would he pay his team to select, edit, and post that sermon clip if not to gain attention and notoriety? It illustrates how a person can effortlessly slander ambition without realizing that we all have desires—many of them good—that we're driven to fulfill. Instead of denying it with false piety, let's be real about it.

In this pastor's defense, his core message wasn't entirely off the mark. He was trying to highlight how people often make life choices—such as dating, relocating to a new city, and so on—without consulting God, only to ask for his blessings afterward. The essence of his message was good. However, there's a huge difference between examining the motives of your ambition and demonizing *all* ambition. If you look more closely at that passage in James, it's *selfish* ambition he calls out. That's where the problem is.

Gazelle Intensity

At times, ambition is *exactly* what's needed to honor God and love your neighbor. There will be seasons in which you need to forge ahead at all costs—when you have to push yourself, when extreme action is necessary, when the so-called work-life balance, though a noble goal, needs to be temporarily set aside. Let me give you an example.

In Proverbs, Solomon gives this advice:

> My son, if you have put up security for your neighbor,
>   if you have shaken hands in pledge for a stranger,
> you have been trapped by what you said,
>   ensnared by the words of your mouth.
> So do this, my son, to free yourself,
>   since you have fallen into your neighbor's hands:
> Go—to the point of exhaustion—
>   and give your neighbor no rest!

> Allow no sleep to your eyes,
>> no slumber to your eyelids.
> Free yourself, like a gazelle from the hand of the hunter,
>> like a bird from the snare of the fowler. (6:1–5)

In this passage, he describes someone trapped by debt. For the person under this crushing weight, Solomon's advice is to make it right as quickly as possible: Better to struggle now and be free than to live perpetually in anxiety. This principle is what Dave Ramsey calls "gazelle intensity,"[1] and it applies to more areas of life than debt. Just as a gazelle flees a lion with life-or-death urgency, sometimes our survival—financial or otherwise—requires intense focus.

It's trendy nowadays to criticize "hustle culture," and I get it. But sometimes godly ambition pushes you to the limit—not because you're irresponsible or self-centered but because you're faithful. Paul expresses his willingness to expend all his energy for the gospel: "Even if I am being poured out like a drink offering on the sacrifice and service coming from your faith, I am glad and rejoice with all of you" (Philippians 2:17). Similarly, he writes to the Corinthians:

> Do you not know that in a race all the runners run, but only one gets the prize? Run in such a way as to get the prize. Everyone who competes in the games goes into strict training. They do it to get a crown that will not last, but we do it to get a crown that will last forever. Therefore I do not run like someone running aimlessly; I do not fight like a boxer beating the air. No, I strike a blow to my body and make it my slave so that after I have preached

to others, I myself will not be disqualified for the prize. (1 Corinthians 9:24–27)

Within the Christian life, there are seasons of gazelle intensity. People will tell you to chill, to slow down, to make less noise. Don't listen. Keep running.

TO BE RICH, OR NOT TO BE RICH?

Confronting the lie that "all ambition is evil" raises a vital question: *Is it wrong for followers of Jesus to be wealthy?* This is a tricky issue because in America, where I live, we're *all* rich by global standards. We tend to think it's the other person who's rich—the one who makes more money or has a nicer car or a bigger house. However, from a global perspective, if you have a roof over your head, clean water to drink, food to eat, and a few luxuries to enjoy, you've been dealt a gracious hand. If you're curious how your income compares with the rest of the world, just enter "How rich am I?" in a search engine and you'll find several fascinating resources to explore.[2]

One of the most famous New Testament stories about wealth is that of the rich young ruler, which appears in three of the Gospels (Matthew 19:16–22; Mark 10:17–22; Luke 18:18–23). It begins with a wealthy young man who approaches Jesus to inquire about what he must do to inherit eternal life. Jesus answers by listing some of the Ten Commandments. "If you want to enter life, keep the commandments," Jesus says (Matthew 19:17).

So far, the young man is on board. He knows he's kept them, so he asks, "What do I still lack?" (verse 20).

And here's where Jesus drops a bomb. "If you want to be

perfect, go, sell your possessions and give to the poor, and you will have treasure in heaven. Then come, follow me" (verse 21).

The young man leaves dejected, because he is very wealthy.

Then Jesus says, "Truly I tell you, it is hard for someone who is rich to enter the kingdom of heaven. Again I tell you, it is easier for a camel to go through the eye of a needle than for someone who is rich to enter the kingdom of God" (verses 23–24).

Let that sink in for a moment. Rather than skirting around Jesus's words, let's face them head-on. According to him, wealth can be a spiritual hazard, a hindrance to heaven. We don't talk about this very much in modern-day America, but as followers of Jesus, let's take our cues from him, not our culture. Our wallets reveal our worship. We like to imagine that we're untethered from our stuff—that if Jesus asked us to give everything away, we'd gladly obey. But speaking for myself, I'm not sure I'd want to hear that instruction. Would you?

LIVING IN THE TENSION

Jesus's message is not that wealthy individuals cannot be saved. Scripture records that people of means were among his disciples, financially supporting his ministry and showing hospitality. Church history overflows with examples of well-off patrons who used their resources to train pastors, fund missionaries, and feed the poor.

Additionally, it's important to remember that the rich young ruler was wealthy *before* he approached Jesus. The text does not specify how he acquired his wealth—whether through hard work, inheritance, or questionable practices. We're not told the backstory, which leaves us in the tension. I think that's exactly where God intends us to be.

Consider two different scriptural directives. On one hand, Jesus said,

> Do not store up for yourselves treasures on earth, where moths and vermin destroy, and where thieves break in and steal. But store up for yourselves treasures in heaven, where moths and vermin do not destroy, and where thieves do not break in and steal. For where your treasure is, there your heart will be also. (Matthew 6:19–21)

Seems pretty straightforward, right? Don't hoard what you have. Prioritize the kingdom, not your bank account. Live for eternal rewards, not material ones.

But on the other hand, there are verses like "A good person leaves an inheritance for their children's children, but a sinner's wealth is stored up for the righteous" (Proverbs 13:22). Scripture affirms that it's wise to save. It's a blessing to the next generations. I resonate with this, as someone who grew up under a Soviet communist regime. Poverty was a crushing reality, and there was little agency to change your situation. Now living in America, I know it's a privilege to provide for my family through hard work. I've committed to living below my means, avoiding debt, and saving diligently. I believe these decisions please God.

We're called to live in the tension of discerning how to live wisely on earth—managing resources and planning for the future—while also ensuring our focus remains on God's eternal kingdom. If money is crowding out the kingdom in your heart, Jesus says to get rid of it. If you seek first the kingdom, you'll be surprised by how your needs are provided for.

As P. T. Barnum once wrote, money "is a very excellent servant but a terrible master."[3] Or as my friend Jason Mayfield insightfully puts it, "Money is a tool. Don't let it master you. Don't you become the tool."

The Antidote: Generosity

If you're sensing that money has a grip on your heart, God *may* prompt you to give away the majority of your assets. He reserves that right. Yet I think he invites most of us to practice consistent generosity instead. There's something about drip-feeding generosity into our lives that shapes our souls over time. It pries our hands off those glittery things we're tempted to chase.

The moment you're comfortable with your income or level of giving, it's probably time to rethink it. The antidote to greed is generosity, and true generosity never slips into mindless autopilot. It stretches you to give more than you thought you could. There's always more to give—whether it's time, talent, or treasure. (For those who just got excited that it's okay to give things other than money, it might be a sign that you should *start* with giving money.)

I don't believe there's a dichotomy between financial success and faithful living. There are individuals at all financial levels who love Jesus and those at all levels who do not. But take Jesus's warning about the deadliness and deceitfulness of wealth seriously, and regularly submit your resources to God. The sting of sacrificial, faith-filled giving leads to joy, not regret.

While the Lord *does* love a "cheerful giver" (2 Corinthians 9:7), in the end, *we* are the ones who end up blessed when we part with our stuff to build God's kingdom.

Let's look now at the second lie about ambition.

LIE 2: AMBITION IS EVERYTHING

"Bro, are you okay?"

My heart pounded as I swerved out of the way, barely missing oncoming traffic. If not for my friend's urgent shout and the panicked honking from the other cars barreling toward us, that might have been the end.

Bleary-eyed, I pulled into a McDonald's for breakfast, thankful to be alive. As the sun crept over the horizon, I felt a tiredness in my soul that I could no longer ignore.

This monthlong tour across the country, hitting colleges and churches to promote my latest musical release, was grueling. Previously, my tours had been brief, allowing me to fly home every few days. This time, the razor-thin margins left no room for such luxuries. It was the longest I'd ever been away from my wife and four-year-old son. The tension in my marriage was growing, and my distance only made it worse.

I was drained in every conceivable way: spiritually, emotionally, relationally, and financially. Still, I felt touring was my only option. I wanted so badly to make it that I was willing to push myself to the point of a mental breakdown, and in my exhausted state, I had put my friend in danger. Something needed to change.

For more than fifteen years, I'd faithfully walked with Jesus. I attended church every Sunday and belonged to a men's small group. Together, we read through the Bible annually multiple times, supported each other, and built a genuine brotherhood. I believed the gospel. Yet despite doing all the "right" things, dysfunction plagued my life—mostly through unhealthy eating habits, a desire for status, and an ongoing struggle with lust.

I was caught in a cycle of frustration and self-destruction. I stayed up every night until around two or three in the morning "working on music," hopped-up on exorbitant amounts of caffeine, sugar, and distractions. I was "busy" but unproductive. Living paycheck to paycheck, I grew depressed, fatigued, and isolated, with no real direction for my career as a rapper in my early thirties.

I knew that this cycle wasn't working, but I didn't know what to do about it. I was certain of God's love, but I also knew he desired more for me—not in a materialistic sense but in a spiritual one, a deeper faithfulness in all aspects of life. Although I had built my faith on the Rock, my daily life felt like sinking sand.

Ambition had become my everything—my North Star. And it was destroying me. As a Christian rapper, I felt I had to hustle to be seen and heard. Those of us who live in America are also conditioned to prioritize our desires and preferences over everything (and everyone) else.

The "ambition is everything" mindset is alive and well in the church. Since their work is done "for God," some people think other divine priorities can take a back seat. This is evident among some Christian rappers I've known and even pastors who chase their ministry goals so fervently that they neglect their own spiritual intimacy with God, their families, and their health—sacrificing these essential elements on the altar of service. Such blurring of lines between doing things *for* God versus doing things *with* God can lead to a perilous trap, subtly distorting one's ministry into something self-serving rather than God-serving.

This reminds me of the biblical principle that "to obey is better than sacrifice" (1 Samuel 15:22). This scripture emphasizes that true adherence to God's will is more crucial than any personal sacrifices we make in his name—especially those he never mandated. At times, I found myself overworking, burning the midnight oil for the sake of ministry, which regrettably came at the cost of valuable family time, robust community engagement, and my own closeness with God. Such scenarios underscore the necessity to balance our ambitions with the overarching command to live according to God's will, ensuring that our efforts in ministry and other pursuits do not overshadow our foundational commitments to faith, family, and personal well-being.

Consider what Scripture calls "selfish ambition." In Greek, it's the term *eritheia,* and it refers to those who snatch what they want by unfair means.[4] It's cutting in line, steamrolling others, and letting jealousy fuel one's actions.

Sometimes Christians try to do big things for the kingdom but in the process become prideful, domineering, and boastful. Cue the narcissistic CEO who neglects his kids and treats people like doormats. Or the pastor who pushes for a new building campaign, even though it will cripple the church's finances and exhaust the staff. It's baptizing our agenda with God's name.

Even Jesus's closest friends struggled with selfish ambition. Right in the middle of the Last Supper, they began arguing about who was the greatest (Luke 22:24). Talk about bad timing. Jesus had just exemplified the greatest act of service by washing their feet, which was normally the job of a slave or "the lowliest of servants."[5] Yet here they were, sparring over who was the best. How easily the attitude of the world seeps into our hearts—even with Jesus close by.

It's easier than we think to approach Jesus with wrong motivation or misguided expectations, even if our aim isn't to chase power or position at others' expense. Like the disciples, I've had many moments when I chased status and success in ways that were destructive. I've tried to further God's kingdom by playing by the world's rules. It never works.

In the mid-2010s, I connected with an influential entrepreneur known for his robust presence in the digital marketing sphere and his relentless pursuit of business success. He was particularly prominent at the time, and having my music featured in his vlogs was a significant achievement. He even followed me on Instagram and would give me a shout-out during his live streams and in the comments section.

Caught up in the whirlwind of social media buzz, I dove headfirst into the hustle culture this entrepreneur championed. I became obsessed with growing my Instagram following. Back then, it was all about crafting the perfect photo and diving deep into analytics—likes, comments, and engagement rates. My efforts seemed to pay off when I got my account verified early on, thanks to a publicist friend with connections. I grew my profile to around fifteen thousand followers.

However, my focus on Instagram "fame" began to overshadow the reason I was on the platform in the first place: my music. In 2017, I launched a project called The Weekly's, where I challenged myself to write, record, and perform a new song in one take every week. While this generated a lot of online attention, it didn't translate into substantial musical progress. I was creating a perception of success that didn't reflect reality. Instead of working to become the kind of artist capable of creating better music, I was chasing the algorithm.

This path led me to profound burnout. The dryness in my soul intensified as I realized that I was chasing status and success at the expense of my art and well-being. Thank God for his mercies, which helped me see that while striving for visibility is valuable, it should never come at the cost of neglecting the real work required to grow and improve as an artist.

In everything you do, there's usually a shortcut available. An easy way that compromises your soul. A type of ambition that puts your own self before others (and God). It's a temptation that promises to deliver everything you want, but it leaves you empty. There's a better way.

A COUNTERCULTURAL AMBITION

The answer is something *between* these two lies—what I call "godly ambition." As a follower of Jesus, you don't have to run from success. Nor should you serve it as an idol. Too many Christians feel ashamed for wanting to accomplish things and rise to the tops of their industries. Or they get caught up in the rat race, forgetting that God's kingdom defines success counterculturally.

Throughout the rest of this book, whenever I use the word *ambition* by itself, I'll be referring to godly ambition. I want you to catch the vision for this.

In the New Testament, the Greek word *philotimeomai* means "to strive earnestly, to aspire, to be ambitious."[6] It shows up three times: In Romans 15:20, Paul talks about his "ambition to preach the gospel where Christ was not known" so he wouldn't be stepping on someone else's turf. The same word is used in 2 Corinthians 5:9 in the context of pleasing God. And in 1 Thessalonians 4:11, the emphasis is on making it our ambition "to lead a quiet life."

A heart for the gospel. A desire to please God. Living a humble life. In a nutshell, that's godly ambition. If I could encapsulate what this type of ambition looks like in a single word, it would be *stewardship*.

AMBITION AS STEWARDSHIP

The problem with worldly ambition is that it leads to entitlement and pride. The "self-made" man, upon achieving his goals, feels he earned them and therefore has no obligation to answer to anyone else. In Scripture, we see a different posture.

Ambition starts with acknowledging that nothing actually belongs to you. Everything is a gift, entrusted to you by God—the creator and owner of all things. "The earth is the LORD's, and everything in it" (Psalm 24:1). Similarly, David prays, "Who am I, and who are my people, that we should be able to give as generously as this? Everything comes from you, and we have given you only what comes from your hand" (1 Chronicles 29:14).

Developing ambition means cultivating a fierce desire to handle those things responsibly—not solely for your benefit but for the Lord's purposes. If a friend asked you to take care of their luxurious mansion while they went on a trip, they'd expect you to maintain their home by not having wild parties, by keeping it tidy, and by bringing in the mail. In much the same way, God expects us to manage the resources he puts in our care.

This responsibility is paradoxical: Our lives are not entirely our own, yet we bear personal responsibility. It's about doing our best with what we've been given, trusting God to guide and teach us along the way. Imagine a gardener nurturing their garden to yield fruit; they must tend to the soil, remove weeds, and protect the plants from pests. However, while the gardener plants and waters, it is ultimately God who brings the harvest.

In the aftermath of my last tour in 2018, I began to reflect on my musical abilities, pondering whether they served a purpose beyond personal gain and provision for my family. I had viewed my music as a tool for sharing my testimony and faith, but a new idea was beginning to take shape—one that would eventually ignite my migration to YouTube. As my fan base grew, a common request among my followers was for feedback on their music. Often, the tracks were rough, and the artists weren't seriously pursuing careers; they were seeking guidance. Inspired by this, I wondered if I could use my experience as a full-time independent musician to offer constructive feedback and career advice. This led to the launch of "Fan Love Fridays," a weekly live stream where I reviewed music submitted by fans. Initially, the reviews were free, but as interest grew, I transitioned the service to my burgeoning Patreon community. For a modest fee of five dollars a month, fans could submit their music for my reaction to it on a live stream. Eventually I enhanced the interaction by allowing them to call in via Zoom for live feedback and advice.

This arrangement proved incredibly beneficial. Not only did it prioritize the needs and growth of my community, but it also encouraged them to take their craft more seriously. Over the years, I witnessed remarkable improvements in the quality of music from these artists, with some even going on to forge successful careers. Many of the artists I met through this stream remain close friends to this day.

This experience profoundly shifted my perspective: I came to see every gift I possess as not merely a means for personal success but also an opportunity to serve others. This is the crux of godly ambition—viewing our talents as tools for stewardship, dedicated to uplifting and aiding others in their own journeys. It's about transforming what we are given into what we can give, making our work not just a career but a calling.

REDEFINING GREATNESS

When you embrace ambition as stewardship, it changes your motivation. Instead of buckling under the pressure to build *your* brand, you become an ambassador for God's kingdom. Your gifts point others to him.

At its core, dominance is a symptom of selfishness and insecurity. Power is a way to prop ourselves up. But as those already loved, redeemed, and adopted into God's family, our acceptance isn't contingent on our success. We're free from the pressure to be the best, even as we give our best.

Let's look again at the scene during the Last Supper when Jesus's disciples are duking it out over status, even as Jesus is moments away from betrayal and crucifixion. Jesus, patient and wise, tells his disciples in response, "The kings of the Gentiles lord it over them; and those who exercise authority over them call themselves Benefactors. But you are not to be like that. Instead, the greatest among you should be like the youngest, and the one who rules like the one who serves. For who is greater, the one who is at the table or the one who serves? Is it not the one who is at the table? But I am among you as one who serves" (Luke 22:25–27).

Jesus doesn't rebuke their desires for greatness; he redefines greatness and redirects them toward *service*. He contrasts the worldly model of leadership, which often involves exerting power over others, with the kingdom model, which is rooted in service and humility. He positions himself as the prime example of this servant leadership, underscoring that true greatness in his kingdom is not about being elevated or having authority over others but about being a servant to all.

In 1 Thessalonians 4:11–12, as part of his emphasis on the importance of leading quiet lives, Paul encourages us to work diligently with our own hands, maintain independence, and demonstrate a life worthy of respect. He posits that it is not merely our words but also the consistent testimony of our lives that draws others to Christ. The apostle Peter echoes this idea: "Live such good lives among the pagans that, though they accuse you of doing wrong, they may see your good deeds and glorify God on the day he visits us" (1 Peter 2:12).

Both Paul and Peter converge on the idea that authentic living—marked by good deeds and a non-dependent lifestyle—does not just earn respect but actively engages the watching world. Through our actions, we embody the church's mission to redeem and reconcile, persuading even skeptics of the genuine nature of our faith. By living exemplary lives, we fulfill our roles within the church as well as extend an invitation to outsiders to witness and eventually glorify God through their own transformations.

Whatever gifts you have are a way to serve others. They're a way to bless the world. You have this pent-up energy and desire for greatness—fantastic! Now channel that into serving others not just where you want to but also where you're needed. Would a friend starting a business benefit from your skills or knowledge? Does a ministry at your church need volunteers? Do you have a dream that would make your neighborhood or city a better place? Could you be the hands and feet of Jesus to someone whom you know is struggling? Look for those sparks—those places God is stirring your heart toward something or someone. Stoke the fire of your ambition.

If nothing comes to mind, that's okay too. This book is designed to help you identify where God might be calling you into action. Stick with me.

God's Pit Crew

It's amazing to see godly ambition in action. For instance, take the story of God's Pit Crew, a Virginia-based nonprofit that began with a simple yet profound vision: to provide disaster relief services to communities in need. In 1999, NASCAR enthusiasts and founders Randy and Terri Johnson saw a parallel between the efficiency of a pit crew during a race and the potential for rapid, organized response to natural disasters. Motivated by their Christian faith, they envisioned a "pit crew for God"—ready at a moment's notice to repair, rebuild, and restore lives affected by disaster.

Volunteers from diverse backgrounds—carpenters, electricians, doctors, and counselors—bring their specific skills, and the organization trains them in disaster response and emotional support, stacking these talents to create a team poised to tackle complex challenges. They exemplify how ambition can transform personal abilities into instruments of divine purpose. Their work not only rebuilds physical structures but also uplifts spirits, helping people see the tangible love of God in action. Through this group's efforts, we witness the true essence of living a life that honors God and embodies the values of his kingdom, serving as a beacon of hope and a testament to the power of faith-driven ambition.

A Prayer for Godly Ambition

Ambition that's surrendered to God's will can change the world. What dreams is God stirring in your heart? As you read this book, let's fan those sparks into a blazing fire. Let's catapult you forward for God's glory. There are things he has put you on earth to do, people he's placed you near to love, and new ventures he's planted in your mind to build.

Before we move on, let's pause and ask God to teach us the difference between selfish ambition and godly ambition. Truth be told, it's easy to mix them up. Even with good intentions, we pursue the right things for the wrong reasons.

Here's a simple prayer as we start this journey together—a way to dedicate your ambition to God:

> **Lord, thank you for creating me with drive, desire, and determination. These are gifts from you to steward. Everything I have, including my time, talent, and treasure, is for your glory. You have gifted me to bless others, so help me live out that high calling.**
>
> **Lord, I know I'm prone to build my own kingdom and promote my own name. I'm hungry for the approval of others. At times I'm addicted to affirmation. Forgive me for the ways I make it about me instead of**

you. Remind me that I was created for your glory. Help me delight in proclaiming your goodness to the world.

I commit to serving others with the gifts you've given me. I have been blessed to be a blessing. I submit to you, Jesus, even when you call me to places and positions I'm reluctant to embrace. I will follow your lead, one step at a time, this day and forever.

Please pour out favor on the work of my hands. Increase my skill and knowledge so I can become excellent in everything I do. Where I lack ambition or am tempted to settle into apathy, stir me to action. Light a fire in my heart to maximize every opportunity, gift, and task for your glory and the good of the world.

Lord, I give all my ambition to you. My life is yours. In Jesus's name, amen.

2

Identity: Know Who You Are

It could have been the best night of my musical career. Instead, it was a train wreck.

In January 2013, I took the stage at the historic House of Blues, where legends like Tupac Shakur—one of my greatest inspirations—had performed. I had just left the rap group the-BREAX to establish my solo career and launch a new label. My ambition was sky-high: to emerge as "the guy" in the solo rap scene. To make it happen, I took on multiple roles—artist, manager, and promoter—juggling full-time work and church responsibilities. Amid this whirlwind of activity, I managed to sell around 400 tickets, and by the time I took the stage, over 650 people were crammed into the venue.

The night began with promise. The opening acts electrified the audience, setting the stage for what should have been the climax of the evening. However, as I took the stage to debut my solo album *Carry On,* the atmosphere shifted. The album was rushed; the songs, unfamiliar to both me and the audience, failed to connect. Although I was backed by a full band and background singers, our performance lacked cohesion—this was our first live rendition of the album, and it showed. By the time my hour-long set ended, I couldn't wait to get off the stage.

With the help of my pastor, I processed what had gone wrong. I was so determined to become a front man that I stopped caring about how my decisions impacted others. In my ambition, I lost myself. What was meant to be a launchpad for my solo career turned into a stark lesson in humility and leadership. From this broken place, I wrote the lyrics to my song "Do for One": "I lost sight of what's in front of me.... My ulterior motives got the best of me.... Trying to reach thousands, but ignoring my community... self-preservation began fueling me."[1]

All of us have moments like this, when ambition shifts from godliness to greed. When we seek our identities apart from Jesus. We're prone to take good gifts—our time, talent, and treasure—and use them to glorify ourselves. We start out with good intentions, but over time, the lure of achievement or glory or pleasure subtly pulls us down a destructive course. By the time we recognize it, the damage has been done.

Throughout my life, I've often found myself ensnared by the lure of my own ambitions. My House of Blues experience didn't instantly cure me of selfish ambition, but it was a pivotal moment that led me to anchor my identity in Christ, not my achievements. Failure was the wake-up call I needed. Although the change didn't happen overnight, that concert marked the beginning of a journey to understand true ambition through the lens of faith.

"There is a way that seems right to a man, but its end is the way to death" (Proverbs 14:12, ESV). A person may believe they should attain as much wealth and status as possible, purely for the sake of it. This belief might even lead the person to make some smart decisions to acquire marketable skills. However, if the ultimate goal is merely to accumulate wealth, it often comes at the expense of other important aspects of life, such as interpersonal relationships or health.

This mindset is prevalent in the hustle culture that dominates many YouTube channels, characterized by a relentless focus on doing more, grinding, and sacrificing sleep. It's epitomized by entrepreneurs who advocate working "your face off" for up to eighteen hours a day."[2] While this approach has led to material success for some, it's also caused family breakdowns and divorce, not to mention anxiety and fatigue.

In retrospect, one must consider whether the pursuit of more money is worth the potential moral and personal fallout. This is reflected in the words of Jesus, "What good will it be for someone to gain the whole world, yet forfeit their soul?" (Matthew 16:26). His question challenges us to weigh the long-term consequences of our beliefs and the true cost of material success.

For the record, I'm not suggesting that if you manage your time, talent, and treasure according to God's ways, fueled by godly ambition, you'll avoid divorce or difficulty. We can't always control others' actions. Marriage, careers, entrepreneurship, and creativity are already challenging, but we shouldn't make them harder than they need to be. Instead, we want to do everything possible to tip the scales in our favor and reduce the risk of moral failure and fallout in the most crucial areas of our lives, specifically marriage and family.

This leads to the Christian perspective that identity is received, not achieved, and is framed by the truths of Scripture rather than the shifting sands of personal or cultural expectations. A Christian's identity is anchored in being a child of God, defined by divine love and purpose instead of societal roles or personal achievements. This foundational identity provides a stable base on which all other aspects of life are built, guiding our actions and choices toward eternal values, not temporal successes.

WHY IDENTITY MATTERS

Who you think you are changes everything. Craig Groeschel once wrote, "What you believe—about who you are and who God is—determines how you behave."[3] In other words, your beliefs about yourself and God shape how you live.

Christians adhere to many truths about God, but faith is not merely about accepting a list of facts—it's about being moved to action. For example, if I firmly believe that increasing physical activity and reducing caloric intake will maintain my health and keep me lean, this belief will influence my behavior. Similarly, if I hold the conviction that living below my means, avoiding debt, and saving diligently will secure my financial freedom, I will naturally align my actions with these beliefs. Belief drives action.

Without a clear sense of your identity in Christ, no amount of success will satisfy you. On the contrary, you'll be tempted to define yourself by what you do, good or bad, rather than looking to who *God* says you are. That's why, right here, at the start of this book, I'm devoting a whole chapter to identity. My hope is to help you anchor your sense of self in Jesus.

The world is happy to offer you a pseudo-identity based on your appearance, income level, or some other external metric. To throw you onto the endless treadmill of performance, always demanding more, never satisfied with who you are. It's tough out there, and many well-meaning Christians have lost themselves despite good intentions. As Scripture says, we must be as gentle as doves but as shrewd as serpents (Matthew 10:16). To that end, it's crucial to anchor your identity in Christ because the winds of life will certainly try to knock you down.

Thankfully, we live in an age that recognizes the importance of identity (even though many may not recognize Christ as the foundation). Modern psychologists and habit-formation experts are now acknowledging what Scripture has long taught us: The beliefs we hold about ourselves and God fundamentally shape our behaviors and life paths.

Atomic Habits by James Clear highlights a pivotal principle: A change in habits and ultimately in life begins with a change in identity. The author argues that people who successfully quit smoking are those who no longer identify as smokers. In other words, to break a habit, you need a new identity. This may sound extreme, but part of the reason we struggle to become the people God calls us to be is that we deal with habit formation on a surface level—a behavioral level—instead of seeking the deep work necessary to change.[4]

THREE ASPECTS OF BEHAVIOR CHANGE

Clear's framework for change consists of three layers: outcomes, processes, and identity.[5] The outer layer, outcomes, is where we typically focus—pursuing desirable goals like losing weight, earning a living, or eating more healthily. The problem is, good intentions aren't enough to achieve these noble goals. Outcomes don't just fall into our laps.

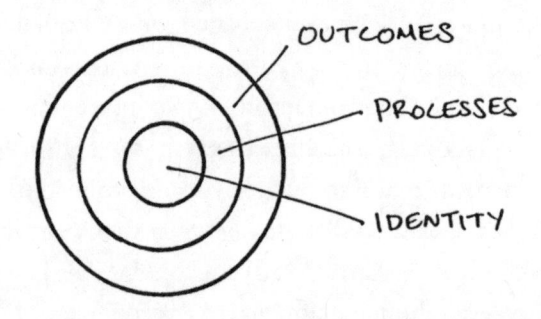

Diagram: Three concentric circles labeled (from outer to inner): OUTCOMES, PROCESSES, IDENTITY.

The second layer is processes. Clear insightfully points out that it's *systems* that determine our success much more than the goals themselves.[6] While everyone aspires to win championships or achieve high levels of success, it's those who develop robust systems and processes, grounded in their well-formed identities, who actually succeed. The key to victory isn't desire alone; it's little daily disciplines that compound to bring big results.

The "third and deepest layer" is identity.[7] Clear rightly says that true change begins *internally,* beginning with how we perceive ourselves. This mirrors the biblical call to see ourselves as new creations in Christ, transformed and called to live out this new identity.

As an athlete, I've applied these principles to my daily routines and choices. For instance, having prepared meals delivered each week from Meal Prep Sunday helps me monitor my diet and get the nutrients I need. Constructing a gym in my backyard has made it easy to exercise consistently. These processes have certainly led to desired outcomes. And I'd encourage you to examine *your* daily rhythms and habits to see if your processes are taking you toward your goals.

I also agree with Clear's framework—that identity is the core of all behavior. However, as a Christian, I wonder, *Where does identity originate?* Clear suggests that identity can be shaped and reshaped through our actions and choices—a concept that holds truth but lacks a foundational anchor from a Christian perspective. As Jesus followers, we don't invent or establish identity through repeated actions; rather, we receive it from God through Jesus Christ. Our Christian identity is rooted in being children of God, redeemed and restored through Christ's sacrifice. We cannot earn or achieve it through our actions; it is a divine gift, immutable and grounded in something far greater than ourselves.

This distinction is crucial because it shifts the basis of identity from our changeable, often unreliable patterns to the unchanging truth of God's Word. Our daily practices and routines, while important, are a *response* to the identity each of us has *already received*, not a means to create it. While Clear's approach empowers individuals to foster change through behavior modification, the Christian approach provides an identity that is both a starting point and a continuous source of inspiration.

If you *really* desire to cultivate godly ambition and make a difference in the world, it all starts with making Christ the foundation of your identity. You must see yourself as God's child before you see yourself as a CEO, creator, teacher, politician, influencer, or [insert your vocation of choice here]. As I shared through my own story of hustling in the music scene at the expense of my soul, it's challenging to anchor one's identity in Christ—especially when the world offers attractive alternatives. To be clear, the alternatives always leave us exhausted, insecure, and empty, but in the real world it's difficult to keep our wits about us. Navigating the complex terrain of identity formation in our overstimulated modern world is no small feat.

So the key question is, *How do we strengthen our identities in*

Christ? How do we suit up and go after our goals without losing ourselves along the way? How do we keep our identities from drifting from Christ into dangerous territory?

Scripture's answer is the principle of replacement.

THE PRINCIPLE OF REPLACEMENT

When trying to reinforce their God-given identities, a lot of Christians fall into the trap of focusing only on defeating sin. The logic goes like this: *If I can just stop doing A, B, and C, I'll become a better person. Just stop sinning!* Naturally, this is a necessary part of following Jesus. Sanctification, the lifelong process of becoming more like Jesus through the power of his Spirit, involves killing sin in our lives.

However, the problem with only targeting sin is that there's a second, equally important side of the equation: *loving God.* To root our identities in God, we can't focus on just what we don't want to do, as if the sum total of Christianity is based on behavior. We're called not only to turn from darkness but also to run toward the light. To swap sin for worship. Avoidance for pursuit. Death for life.

So if you want to strengthen your identity in Christ, run *from* sin and *toward* God at the same time. The apostle Paul mentions both actions: "Throw off your old sinful nature and your former way of life, which is corrupted by lust and deception. Instead, let the Spirit renew your thoughts and attitudes" (Ephesians 4:22–23, NLT). This language of throwing off and putting on has been called the "principle of replacement."[8]

Picture yourself in a dirty old T-shirt, right after a long jog in the summer heat. You're about to head out for a nice dinner, so after removing the smelly shirt and taking a quick shower, you put on a fresh, clean T-shirt. This process of removing what's soiled and putting on what's new is what God desires to do in our lives every day. It is the process of sanctification. One step at a time, he strips off the old and gives us the new.

You may be thinking, *Wait, I thought God made me new when I came to faith in Christ. Am I somehow not fully saved?* Let me be clear: The moment you trusted in Jesus, God instantly saved you, securing your place in his kingdom. However, it takes a lifetime to adjust to this new reality. God, in his kindness, welcomes us in our messy state, and he's patient enough to refine us for the duration of our lives. As he renews us piece by piece, we start to look and sound more like him. We could never do this transforming work on our own. We need the Holy Spirit, whom God has graciously given to all who believe in him.

In Christ, you are a new creation who is renewed every day. This is possible because he's made his home in you. When God moves in, positive change happens. He transforms us from the inside out.

For a moment, let's zoom in on the two aspects of putting off sin and putting on holiness. Both are essential if you want to strengthen your identity in Christ and go about doing his good work in the world.

PUTTING OFF SIN, PUTTING ON HOLINESS

One of the hardest parts of following Christ is defeating sin habits—especially those that have existed for years. As you pursue godly ambition and steward your gifts well to make an impact, nothing will derail you faster than unaddressed sin habits.

When I first encountered Jesus's teachings on relationships, marriage, and lust, I was challenged. Initially, I started going to church only to spend summers with a Christian girl I was dating, thinking, *Why not?* However, as I continued attending, my heart slowly shifted toward the gospel, and I became more open to following God. But then I faced God's standards for relationships—specifically, no sex outside of marriage—which was a massive shift from what I wanted and expected. I also learned that from a Christian worldview anchored in Scripture, the unborn have value. This meant that if my girlfriend and I were to slip up and she became pregnant, abortion was not an option.

Things became even more challenging when I discovered that consuming pornography was not permissible either. I had figured that since I couldn't have sex with my girlfriend outside of marriage, I would just consume porn to hold myself over. However, Jesus's teaching that "anyone who looks at a woman lustfully has already committed adultery with her in his heart" hit me hard (Matthew 5:28). Consuming explicit material, even while being celibate, was not an option. This revelation forced me to confront and rethink my entire approach to managing sexual desire under God's guidance.

The paradigm shift from sin to holiness wasn't easy for me. I grappled with God's design for sexuality, wondering why it had to be restricted, much like a child might question why they can't have ice cream every night. My previous belief was that true freedom meant no restraints, allowing for the pursuit of whatever felt good. But as I delved deeper into Scripture, my understanding of freedom evolved—it meant not just erasing constraints but also recognizing that self-control would bring a new joy and peace I'd never known. I began to see that although God's standards for sexuality felt stringent to a young man full of hormones, they were far from unreasonable. The more I considered the potential impact of adopting God's sexual ethics—avoiding pornography and waiting until marriage for sex—the more I saw their benefits for me and for others. Slowly, one step at a time, I was putting off sin.

Here's another example. Before I was a Christian, I thought that I could do whatever I wanted with my money and that maybe if I had a little left over, I would save some for a rainy day. The objective was to get the nicest things, even if that meant living above my means by committing to a car payment that I couldn't afford or financing expensive tennis shoes with a credit card that I didn't really need (real examples, I regret to say). I figured it would all work out later. I didn't understand that God had entrusted me with worldly wealth to bless others and bring him glory by living below my means, saving, giving generously, and being faithful with what I'd been given.

Much like God's sexual standards, these financial principles initially felt counterintuitive. I questioned why God placed such importance on how I managed my finances. Yet considering the broader implications, I pondered, *What if everyone lived within their means, saved diligently, and gave generously? How might the world transform?* These principles, though countercultural, began to transform me.

Trusting and applying Jesus's teachings about money and other areas of my life have deepened my faith and confirmed the trustworthiness of God's wisdom. Because my foundation was strong, I could build more of my life on it. In other words, I was putting on holiness. That's not to say I am perfect—*far* from it. But the more I give myself to God's Word and put it into practice, the more my identity is anchored in him. And it's the same for you.

REHEARSE YOUR IDENTITY

The enemy wants to distort your identity. To tempt you to define yourself by your appearance, your accomplishments, or even your failures. In my experience, one of Satan's favorite tactics is to get you to abuse ambition—to lose yourself in the pursuit of great things and life's distractions. He even uses things you're doing "for God." Our status in Christ doesn't change; our *perception* does. Like Peter walking toward Jesus across the water's surface, we lose sight of Jesus and, in the process, lose ourselves.

One of the best ways I've found to rehearse my identity in Christ—to remind myself that I belong to him alone—is to read scriptures that proclaim this truth. Scripture is a gift: It offers a panoramic view of our status as God's beloved children. God's will is found in God's ways, and God's ways are found in God's Word.

To grow in Christ, we must listen to the Word more than the world. We must cling to what the Scriptures say about our identities. The Bible is *filled* with declarations about who we are in Christ. Soak in these truths. Write them on note cards, and carry them with you. Write them on sticky notes, and post them on your bathroom mirror, dashboard, or fridge. Memorize them with a friend or your family. Meditate on them "day and night" (Psalm 1:2). As Moses instructed in Deuteronomy, "These commandments that I give you today are to be on your hearts. Impress them on your children. Talk about them when you sit at home and when you walk along the road, when you lie down and when you get up. Tie them as symbols on your hands and bind them on your foreheads. Write them on the doorframes of your houses and on your gates" (6:6–9). In my prayer journal, I pick a new memory verse every week or two. I write it down every day while saying it out loud. It's a practice that anchors my soul, reminding me that I am who *God* says I am.

This habit may seem basic, but don't underestimate the power of surrounding yourself with God's Word. The Bible is a massive book, I know, so if you're looking for a simple way to start, here's an excerpt from a list of verses compiled by author Neil T. Anderson that declare aspects of your Christ-given identity. As you read through the list, start with the words *God says* . . .

I Am Accepted
John 1:12—I am God's child.
John 15:15—I am Christ's friend.
Romans 5:1—I have been justified.
1 Corinthians 6:17—I am united with the Lord, and I am one spirit with Him.
1 Corinthians 6:20—I have been bought with a price. I belong to God.
1 Corinthians 12:27—I am a member of Christ's Body.
Ephesians 1:1—I am a saint.
Ephesians 1:5—I have been adopted as God's child.

I Am Secure
Romans 8:1–2—I am free from condemnation.
Romans 8:28—I am assured all things work together for good.
Romans 8:31–34—I am free from any condemning charges against me.
Romans 8:35–39—I cannot be separated from the love of God.

2 Corinthians 1:21–22—I have been established, anointed and sealed by God.

Philippians 1:6—I am confident that the good work God has begun in me will be perfected.

Philippians 3:20—I am a citizen of heaven.

I Am Significant

Matthew 5:13–14—I am the salt and light of the earth.

John 15:1, 5—I am a branch of the true vine [Jesus], a channel of His life.

John 15:16—I have been chosen and appointed to bear fruit.

Acts 1:8—I am a personal [Spirit-empowered] witness of Christ.

1 Corinthians 3:16—I am God's temple.

2 Corinthians 5:17–21—I am a minister of reconciliation for God.

2 Corinthians 6:1—I am God's co-worker (see 1 Corinthians 3:9).[9]

I encourage you to read through this list once a day. Or write out one of these verses each day, then read it several times as you go through your routine. Remind yourself, again and again, how God sees you. You will need these reminders as you step out, take risks, and use your gifts for the kingdom. As you pursue godly ambition, don't let the enemy twist your goals or whisper lies about who you are. If you've trusted in Jesus, you are his. End of story.

Not only are we made with extraordinary care and purpose; we are also equipped and destined to glorify God in unique ways. Knowing this can empower and motivate us to seek out and fulfill those purposes, understanding our lives as intricately woven parts of God's greater plan.

Once you know *who* you are in Christ, figuring out *what* you're here to do is a lot easier. God has placed you on this earth for a reason, so let's find out what that reason is.

3

Calling: Know Why You're Here

The pressure to find your calling can feel overwhelming. No question has higher stakes than *Why do I exist?* We often think about a calling like it's a secret blueprint God has laid out for each of us. One wrong decision, and the whole thing collapses. But God isn't playing games with you. He's not leaving clues, expecting you to put them together or else. His plan for you isn't ruined by layoffs, dead-end jobs, sudden career shifts, or health challenges.

Think of calling not as a prediction of the future but as a *process*—something God reveals and confirms over time. Isn't that relieving? You don't have to figure it out all at once. God, in his kindness, reveals our paths one step at a time, in ways and timing we can handle. Settle in for the journey, knowing he's in control.

Calling is often equated with God's will for our lives. Again, God's will is found in God's ways, which are found in God's Word. When you think about your calling, instead of focusing on the destination, focus on aligning yourself with God's ways and asking how you're doing on the journey. Why are you on the journey? What if the *how* and *why* matter more than the *what*?

Still, the question remains: Where do we start to discern his specific callings for our lives? Some of you need a first step. A sense of direction. Or maybe you're weighing a bunch of options, looking for God's guidance on which one to go all-in on.

As a high school senior, I gave a presentation (worth a huge portion of my English grade) about a career path I wanted to pursue. Though unconventional, my hypothetical career was to run an independent record label. My teachers were half-puzzled, half-impressed by my choice. Here's the crazy thing: A few years after high school, I actually started that label, eventually building it into a full-time job. Turns out, some high school assignments actually shape your future. I encourage every young person to dream about the future—to think deeply about how God has wired them. Plans change, naturally. But it's wise to continually seek the Lord's direction, asking him to reveal our next steps.

Fast-forward to today. I'm still involved in the music industry, but it's no longer my main focus. Life throws curveballs. Like mine, your journey will have unexpected shifts, setbacks, and surprises. Whether you've always known what you want to do for a living or you're a late bloomer like me, God often reveals our paths one step at a time.

This is a good thing. It means you have freedom to explore, fail, try new things, and discern where God is leading you. So, the pressure's off. You can breathe.

The process of finding your calling can be complex and confusing, so let's start by defining some terms.

YOUR PURPOSE

To start, I want to explore three words that will be helpful as you discern God's call on your life: *purpose, assignment,* and *call-*

ing. These words are used synonymously in popular Christian vocabulary, but since that gets messy, let's unravel them.

We'll begin with *purpose*. In America, where we process life more as individuals than as a collective group, it's common to focus on "my purpose." However, part of following Christ is belonging to a family. As in any family, we don't have the right to operate however we want as individuals; instead, we contribute to the good of the whole. Additionally, life is not primarily about *me*; it's about *us*. Scripture says that *all* of God's people have the same ultimate purpose: to know God and make him known.

This should excite you. You're part of a narrative far grander than any individual story. Realizing that your purpose is to know God and make him known isn't about diminishing your role but about embracing a mission that expands into eternity. For most of us, it's a paradigm shift to realize life is about God, not us. Even as Christians, it's easy to forget this in a world that endlessly appeals to our self-centeredness through marketing and media.

Sometimes, we struggle with the idea of glorifying God with our lives because we've embraced Christian platitudes and slogans that misconstrue God as a genie who exists merely to fulfill our whims. We're wired to think that the universe revolves around us, that we're unique snowflakes at the center of the narrative. Fighting this impulse is a full-time job. If we're honest, it feels like a loss to give up the spotlight, even to God. Now add in ambition—the desire to make a difference in the world by pursuing excellence with our skills—and the potential for misunderstanding our purpose grows exponentially.

We misquote passages like Psalm 37:4, claiming that God "will give you the desires of your heart" without connecting it to the stipulation in the first part of the verse: "Take delight in the LORD." And we forget (or intentionally leave out) the next verse, "Commit your way to the LORD; trust in him, and he will act" (verse 5, ESV). Thus, the promise of God granting us the desires of our hearts is contingent on our trust in him, our delight in him, and our commitment to letting him lead.

While many of us struggle with some degree of "main character syndrome,"[1] Scripture declares that *God* is the main character in the story of the universe. The more we accept this and *delight* in it, the more our sense of purpose grows. Why would our souls delight in life being more about God than about us? Because we are wired to glory in something greater than ourselves. To stand in awe of ultimate greatness. We were made to worship the Lord of heaven and earth.

Here are a few passages that express our collective calling to know God and make him known:

> The earth is the LORD's, and everything in it,
>   the world, and all who live in it. (Psalm 24:1)

> You are worthy, our Lord and God,
>   to receive glory and honor and power,
> for you created all things,
>   and by your will they were created
>   and have their being. (Revelation 4:11)

> Whether you eat or drink or whatever you do, do it all for the glory of God. (1 Corinthians 10:31)

> From him and through him and for him are all things.
>   To him be the glory forever! Amen. (Romans 11:36)

> When you produce much fruit, you are my true disciples. This brings great glory to my Father. (John 15:8, NLT)

> Don't you realize that your body is the temple of the Holy Spirit, who lives in you and was given to you by God? You do not belong to yourself, for God bought you with a high price. So you must honor God with your body. (1 Corinthians 6:19–20, NLT)

YOUR ASSIGNMENT

A less-used but equally important word is *assignment*. And no, I'm not talking about the homework you received in middle school. While all believers have a shared purpose, every disciple has a unique job to do, here and now. This is your assignment, where God currently has you. It can include your job—what you do to pay the bills. Or it could be parenting little ones. Your assignment is what you spend the majority of your time doing, whether or not it brings a paycheck. Unlike your purpose (which never changes), your assignment can shift with the seasons of life. For instance, you might be called to give most of your time to nursing babies and wrangling toddlers right now, but with time, this season will end. God will then give you a new assignment. Or perhaps your current assignment is your job. You might work in that role for the next few years but then find God transitioning you to a new assignment after that. The key is to accept your assignment in this season and give yourself fully to it. It requires openhandedness and trust, knowing that God switches our focus according to his timing and wisdom.

I want to tell you about my friend Willie. As I was growing up in San Diego, my dad wasn't in my life, which led to me getting into a lot of trouble. I got arrested at the age of eleven and had to do some community service. Thankfully, my next-door neighbors were two gentlemen, Charles and Willie, who went to a local church where I ended up doing a lot of my community service hours. Willie became like a father to me. He'd pick me up in his semi, take me on short trips, and share the gospel with me. Although his assignment in those days was to drive trucks for a living, it didn't define everything in his life. Willie knew that his purpose was so much greater than his day job—it involved exemplifying the gospel with his actions, including being a father figure to me when I really needed one.

The lesson is this: While your assignment in this season is a gift from God, there are many other ways to live out your purpose. He's put people in your life to disciple and given you the means to serve your neighbor.

PURPOSE VS. ASSIGNMENT

I've had lots of jobs in my life—at Pizza Hut, where my culinary "skills" were put to the test; as a church janitor, where I learned the humility of doing unrecognized work; at the YMCA, where I became an expert at navigating noisy teens; and as an aide to adults with disabilities, where I learned the value of patience and compassion. Through all these assignments, my purpose remained constant: *to know God, love him, and share his love with others.* The assignments varied, but my purpose did not.

One pitfall of focusing too much on your assignment is that it can lead to a sense of disillusionment or dissatisfaction when your role changes or when things don't go as planned. By contrast, understanding your purpose, which remains constant, allows you to navigate these changes with a sense of peace and confidence. "We know that in all things God works for the good of those who love him, who have been called according to his purpose" (Romans 8:28). It's so freeing to realize you can't outmaneuver God's wisdom. Transitions and setbacks happen, but no matter what comes, there's *always* an opportunity to live out your purpose and give glory to him.

Now that we understand purpose and assignment, let's unpack the third term: *calling*. What is your calling, and how do you discover it?

HOW TO FIND YOUR CALLING

Early in my Christian walk, I viewed God's will for my life as a destination, involving a sort of scavenger hunt to find the secret location that held the keys to my future. Unfortunately, I think many Christians also think this way. Each obsesses over their "calling" like it's a map they must follow step-by-step or else life goes sideways. To them, only the faithful find their callings, while everyone else stumbles around in the dark, banging their heads against the wall and hitting endless dead ends. Meanwhile, supposedly God sits back and enjoys the show, shaking his head in disapproval. Friends, this is not the heart of God. He's kind. He *wants* you to find your way; in fact, he's your Good Shepherd who delights to guide you. God isn't playing games with your destiny—that's not his nature.

God's calling is not one secret path to discover; it's the culmination of everything God has placed in your life, including your desires. Like your purpose, your calling is bigger than one role or vocation. And like your assignment, it's related to your gifts and opportunities. In a way, your calling is where purpose (to glorify God) and assignment (specific roles) overlap.

It's taken me years to learn this, and I want to save you that heartache. If you feel confused about your calling and unsure where to start, take heart! You're not alone. The process of discerning your calling can take a long time—even decades. However, it's not something to stress about; it's something to thoughtfully pray through as you recognize patterns in your life. I recommend asking three key questions to discern your calling:

1. What do I love doing? (passion)
2. How do my gifts meet the world's needs? (mission)
3. What can I get paid to do? (vocation)

Let's walk through these three questions one at a time.

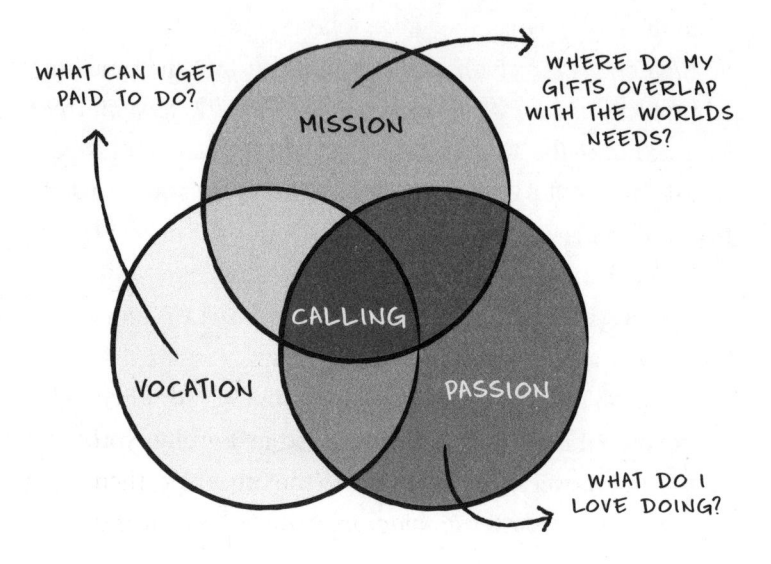

Passion: What Do You Love Doing?

Too often we follow the mantra that happiness is based on finding something we love so much that we'd do it for free. Many public figures, celebrities, influencers, and CEOs encourage us to follow our passions.

Jocko Willink says, "I definitely think the best thing to do is work at a job that you're passionate about and make a lot of money."[2]

Steve Jobs seems to echo this viewpoint: "You have to have a lot of passion for what you're doing.... The reason is because it's so hard that if you don't, any rational person would give up."[3]

But the truth is, it doesn't always work that way. Sometimes people achieve their goals and still feel empty. Not to mention the millions of people who don't get the luxury of choosing their jobs—they're just trying to survive. It feels unfair to say that only those with the freedom to choose their vocations can find their true callings.

Also, the reality is that being passionate about something doesn't mean you have a shot at doing it. Mike Rowe, former host of *Dirty Jobs,* gives the example of someone who is passionate about becoming an astronaut. They might even start pursuing it, but Rowe warns:

> Statistically, you're not going to make it. You know why? Because there are only like a hundred astronauts. Tough! It's a tough thing to do. I think when you put passion first, you erect a giant wall. If you can get over it and get down to the other side, then you get to write the biography and tell the world

about how you identified your wish.... In my view, that's simply not how most success works.... Never follow your passion, but always bring it with you.[4]

Instead of directing us to choose between a life driven by passion and a life bound by practicality, Scripture encourages us to hold these two things in tension. Unlike the "do whatever makes you happy" philosophy of modern America, the Bible denies that passion is everything. Passion matters, as we'll see in a moment, but it's not the be-all and end-all of the Christian life. For starters, Jesus is abundantly clear that hard times will befall his friends:

> Whoever wants to be my disciple must deny themselves and take up their cross and follow me. For whoever wants to save their life will lose it, but whoever loses their life for me will find it. What good will it be for someone to gain the whole world, yet forfeit their soul? Or what can anyone give in exchange for their soul? (Matthew 16:24–26)

Sometimes following Jesus means carrying your cross and crucifying your passions. It requires dying to your hopes and dreams, only to have them replaced by even greater ones. To follow him requires total surrender. Going places we would never go on our own. Choosing obedience over preference.

Another pushback to the idea that "passion is everything" is that we can't always trust our own desires or judgments. "The heart is deceitful above all things and beyond cure. Who can understand it?" (Jeremiah 17:9). Jesus says, "What comes out of a person is what defiles them. For it is from within, out of a person's heart, that evil thoughts come.... All these evils come from inside and defile a person" (Mark 7:20–23).

"Many are the plans in a person's heart, but it is the LORD's purpose that prevails" (Proverbs 19:21). When I came to faith, I was already making music, so my goal was to become a rap star for Jesus. I was certain this would be my career path. I was passionate about it. I was willing to suffer for it. I was willing to do everything I could to hone my skills. I don't think anyone was more devoted to sharing the gospel as a rapper, *and yet* my career has taken me in an entirely different direction. I still love music, write songs, and produce for other artists when I can, but it's more of a side hustle now.

While there are good reasons to keep your passions in perspective, you should also pay attention to them. God has wired you to love, excel at, and long for certain things. He's prepared good works in advance for you to do as someone created in his image. And he's given you *desires* for those good works. In some Christian circles, feelings are demonized, as if obedience never aligns with what we actually want. That's not true. If the Spirit who raised Christ Jesus lives in you, of course he's stirring up your heart, nudging you to use your gifts.

What captures your imagination? What stirs your spirit? Maybe you're passionate about feeding the poor, collecting vintage comic books, playing basketball, sewing, creating apps, writing poetry, solving financial problems, or ministering to the elderly. Nothing is too small to make a difference in God's kingdom. My advice is to pay attention to those things you feel born to do. Your interests are no coincidence; they've been placed within you by your Creator.

Passion and Pain

What if I told you there's a different definition of *passion*—that it's more congruent with what the Scriptures teach us about life, purpose, meaning, and our assignment on this side of eternity?

Before moving on, it's important to clarify that having a passion for something doesn't always mean it will be fun or easy. Passion isn't about doing whatever you want. It's about what you're willing to suffer for. If you really want to know what you care about, consider what you're willing to sacrifice for. In an interview, Jerry Seinfeld said, "Your blessing in life is when you find the torture you're comfortable with."[5]

Choosing your vocation is not about finding something you love to do so much that you'd do it for free and if you can make money from it, whoop-de-do. No, find something you're so passionate about that you're willing to sacrifice yourself for it. To lay down your life for it. To endure agony. It's not about "never working a day in your life"; it's about finding so much meaning in your work that you allow the work to transform you. "If you do what is easy, your life will be hard. But if you do what is hard, your life will be easy."[6] Passion allows us to choose the hard things in life so that over the long haul, life will become easier. Don't separate passion from pain. If you honor your passions, expect the road to be rewarding but not easy.

If you're trying to discern your assignment in this season, ask yourself, *What am I willing to sacrifice for? What am I willing to lay down in the short term to accomplish in the long term?*

Some of us want to go out and change the world and help usher in the kingdom of heaven on this side of eternity. But perhaps we're lacking some of the practical skills required to do what we're supposed to do. Transitioning from a rapper to a YouTuber meant I needed to make up for a skill deficit—there were new software, hard skills, and things about cameras and lighting to learn. Because I had a deep passion, I was willing to sacrifice in the short term to make a long-term impact.

If passion involves embracing suffering and agony, don't be surprised or discouraged when you start something new and it's hard. How do you fight discouragement? You have to sacrifice pleasure, the things that feel good in the short term. Jesus endured the agony of crucifixion because he had a more powerful long-term vision: "For the joy set before him he endured the cross, scorning its shame, and sat down at the right hand of the throne of God. Consider him who endured such opposition from sinners, so that you will not grow weary and lose heart" (Hebrews 12:2–3).

None of us will ever experience the depths of pain Jesus felt on the cross; however, his example shows us the importance of laying aside temporary comfort for a greater purpose. It's no accident that if you look up the word *passion* in the *Oxford Dictionary of English*, the second definition refers to "the suffering and death of Jesus."[7] He shows us that passion and pain intermingle for the most beautiful life imaginable. Again, I'm not putting our work on the same level as Jesus's. But as his disciples, we should follow his example by accepting pain as a natural part of doing great things for the kingdom. When you're tempted to abandon your passions because the road gets tough, look to Jesus and keep going. Don't lose heart.

MISSION: HOW DO YOUR GIFTS OVERLAP WITH THE WORLD'S NEEDS?

The second thing to consider when discerning your calling is this: *How do my gifts overlap with the world's needs?*

I first met my friend Trizzle, a former orthopedic surgeon, through our shared love for music. Once, when I asked how he ended up going into medicine, he responded, "It was a desire for security. When I was younger, during the 2008 recession, my family did really well at first. But then, we got everything stripped from us. We lost our house, my dad lost his job, and my parents got divorced. So, my entire upbringing was taken from me."

After becoming a surgeon, even while working sixty to seventy hours a week, Trizzle couldn't shake his passion for fitness. "Even though I was working in the ICU, I still worked out five times a week. People in the hospital were like, 'How are you getting these workouts in?'" On top of that, he had begun his own business training fifty to sixty people at the gym.

He managed to juggle this packed schedule for a time, but one day he had a panic attack while on a run. "I had so much pressure and so much demand.... Eventually, I just didn't have the energy for my wife or at home," he explained.

His wife gave him an ultimatum: "You have to make this decision. You can't hold on to both things."

When he realized he had to choose between his vocation and his passion, he experienced a breakthrough. "I made my two-month salary in one week with my business while working full-time at my job," he said. "That's when I knew fitness was where I needed to be."

Making this leap wasn't easy. Trizzle shared, "My parents

questioned my decision, saying, 'You went to school for eight years. You took out $250,000 in student loans, and you're gonna give that up for this?' But my wife saw what I was going through and supported me in making the change." Even though it was risky, Trizzle knew this was the right path.

Now Trizzle serves as a father to the fatherless, fostering children through his church. He told me, "My church is really passionate about foster care. We've had about three or four foster children. Our goal is to have over twenty-five foster families in our church." This resonates with Matthew 25, where Jesus teaches about serving the "least of these." Trizzle's story shows that when we align our ambitions with God's purpose, we find more fulfillment than we ever imagined. Trizzle's purpose remained the same in Christ, but his assignment changed.

I love how his story showcases the collision of passion and mission. As an avid athlete, he maintained his workout regimen despite a demanding career as a surgeon. God gifted him physically, and the more he nurtured that gift, the more he realized he could meet the needs of others looking to get in better shape.

As you seek out your calling, consider how God has gifted you. Where do you excel? What skills have you worked hard to cultivate? What abilities come naturally to you? Pay attention to those areas, and look for ways to serve others with those abilities. In the overlap of your gifts and the world's need, you will find your calling.

Vocation: What Can You Get Paid to Do?

The third and final thing to consider when discerning your calling is, *What can I get paid to do?* Your vocation may not be a paid role (stay-at-home parents, I'm looking at you). But it often is. Be practical: What opportunities are actually presenting themselves to you right now?

The tension lies in the thought, *But what if I'm stuck in a job I hate, where I have zero passion?* I hear you. We don't always get to choose our jobs. Still, God calls us to be faithful. Without the lessons you're learning now, you won't be ready for what's next. Be patient. Trust God.

In the early stages of my career, navigating the balance between passion, mission, and vocation was hard. I realized you can't always have all three in a job, so you must choose what best suits your needs and goals at any given time. During this phase, I chose to work with adults with developmental disabilities. It was incredibly fulfilling and easy in terms of workload. It allowed me to be fully present with my clients, assisting them with daily activities like going to appointments, the gym, and school. The work provided a stable and predictable schedule, which was a huge plus.

The trade-off, however, was the pay—it wasn't great. But this was a strategic choice for me. The job's low demands and stable hours freed up my afternoons and evenings, giving me the precious time from three to six to pursue music and other passions. This setup was ideal for cultivating new skills and bridging gaps in areas I was passionate about, which I believed were important in the world.

Jonathan Pageau, a Christian iconographer, artist, and author, follows this reasoning as well. In a conversation I had with him, he discussed the necessity for creatives to embrace a simpler, more frugal lifestyle to pursue their artistic passions fully. Jonathan's approach involves living below his means so he can devote himself entirely to his art. This lifestyle choice, though humble, is actually about prioritizing long-term fulfillment and creative freedom over immediate financial gain. Such choices underscore the importance of distinguishing our self-worth from our income, recognizing that our value extends far beyond our professional roles.

Embracing a season of earning less to focus on personal growth and development is a challenging decision, especially in a culture where so much of one's identity is tied to income. However, what you do for work does not define who you are. It's merely one way you contribute to the world. Choosing to take a step back financially to enhance personal and creative skills can be a profound investment in your future. Perhaps God is calling you to stay in a low-paying job because that's exactly where he wants you to serve. It's easy nowadays to assume there's something better around the corner—an opportunity that will make you rich or remove the stress from your life. This may be the case, but there's also a good chance God wants you to be faithful over the long haul. To use your gifts in humble ways. This might sound disappointing to the world, but for those walking with Christ, nothing is more fulfilling than feeling God's pleasure and seeing lives changed.

WOUNDS AND WORK

In a broken world, one of the greatest temptations we face is to work *for* love rather than *from* love. Friend, don't try to curate your calling to fill the void in your soul. Many people enter fields like music, media, or sports looking for attention and validation. They need success to feel complete. This is a dangerous game.

If your sense of calling stems from a place of brokenness

rather than godly ambition, you'll run yourself into the ground. Indeed, there are fates worse than failing to achieve success. What good is it to gain the world but forfeit your soul? To stockpile earthly goods but miss out on heaven? To achieve glory for yourself while missing out on the thrill of glorifying the One who made you? If you have unresolved hurt or trauma, don't glaze over it. Beyond growing up without a dad and getting into trouble with the law, I was sexually assaulted by some neighbors as a boy. This experience left a horrible hole in my soul, and it's taken years of prayer, counseling, and support to heal. Some days, I still feel like I'm healing. The point is, though your past doesn't define you, it *does* impact how you see the world. Be mindful that your wounds need proper care. Medicating through achievement never works.

As you discern your calling, I encourage you to search your soul. Sift your motives. Pay attention to those pain points that will hijack your ambition. As followers of Jesus, our greatest hope—and what keeps our ambition in check—is the love and grace of Jesus. In him, we are accepted, adopted, forgiven, and being renewed. God accepts you on the basis of Christ's sacrifice, so breathe easy. You no longer have to chase recognition, fame, or success. You don't have to impress God; you just have to *receive* him.

One of my favorite descriptions of God's love comes from Deuteronomy 7, where God expresses his unconditional love for Israel:

> The LORD did not set his affection on you and choose you because you were more numerous than other peoples, for you were the fewest of all peoples. But it was because the LORD loved you and

> kept the oath he swore to your ancestors that he brought you out with a mighty hand and redeemed you from the land of slavery, from the power of Pharaoh king of Egypt. Know therefore that the LORD your God is God; he is the faithful God, keeping his covenant of love to a thousand generations of those who love him and keep his commandments. (verses 7–9)

God *is* love, so he needs no special reason to set his affection on you. In the New Testament, he expresses his love for you using the same terminology he used to dote on Israel: "You are a chosen people, a royal priesthood, a holy nation, God's special possession, that you may declare the praises of him who called you out of darkness into his wonderful light" (1 Peter 2:9).

As you seek clarity on your calling, start here: *You are loved by Jesus.* Let that truth sink deep into your bones. Let it inspire you to surrender control, slow down to heal, embrace challenges, live below your means (if necessary), and lead a quiet life.

CONSIDER YOUR CALLING

I know this is a lot to take in, so let's hit pause. Right now, I want you to take a deep breath and give yourself space to reflect on these three questions:

1. What do I love doing? (passion)
2. Where do my gifts overlap with the world's needs? (mission)
3. What can I get paid to do? (vocation)

Use a journal or digital document to record your thoughts. As you do, bring your ideas, hopes, and questions to God in prayer. I've found it's also important to bring others into this conversation about calling, whether it be your spouse, mentor, friend, or small group. It can be so illuminating to process life with others—to ask them what gifts and opportunities they see in you. This type of community is God's gift to you (more on that in chapter 10).

As we continue this journey together, I pray your calling becomes clearer. I've written every chapter to help you listen for God's voice, take practical steps forward, and move further into God's plan for you.

In the next chapter, I want to help you make sense of the season you're in. If you're currently feeling unsure about the future or stagnant in your current role, there are important lessons God wants you to learn. So, let's dive in.

PART 2

Cultivate Your Growth

Master the Fundamentals

So far, if you're tracking with me, you have a vision for godly ambition. You're fired up to use your time, treasure, and talent for the good of the world. Your identity is rooted in Christ, and you're gaining a clearer sense of your calling.

There's just one problem: You hate your job right now.

Or maybe you enjoy your work, but it barely pays your rent.

Or perhaps you've been considering a next step but lack the needed credentials or skills.

It's easy to talk about ambition, identity, and calling in *theory*, but in the real world, practical needs eat dreams for breakfast. Most of us can't walk away from our responsibilities to chase our dream jobs. Many of us are terrified to take the leap, afraid that we'll crash and burn. If you feel frustrated, held back, bored, or restless where you are, I want to offer some unconventional advice: *Settle in.*

I don't say this to dismiss your frustration. When I served as a church janitor, there were moments I resented the work while scrubbing toilets on my hands and knees. It was humbling. It wasn't the path I would have chosen, but it was fertile ground for Jesus to work in me. It's the same for you. God works in the waiting: in the unseen, unsexy, everyday grind. He's placed you here—perhaps not forever, but here nonetheless. Your circumstances are under his watchful eye. He knows what you need.

In seasons when I just wanted to move on to the next thing, two truths have anchored me: *Work to eat,* and *sow to reap.*

WORK TO EAT

"The one who is unwilling to work shall not eat" (2 Thessalonians 3:10). I love that Scripture isn't lofty or idealistic; it's gritty, written from the trenches of real life. The truth is, we all have to pay the bills. Period. Sometimes, like it nor not, this means working a nine-to-five. Clocking in and out. Pulling the graveyard shift. Developing a side hustle to make ends meet. Or keeping the cushy job that doesn't challenge you because you're supporting your family. The struggle is real, and the Bible is honest about that.

In case that sounds depressing, rest assured that your daily work—mind-numbing as it may be—is a blessing. It's not perfect, but it's a privilege to provide for yourself and those you love. Putting food on the table honors God. It's noble to give your best at work. Scripture says, "Whatever you do, work at it with all your heart, as working for the Lord, not for human masters" (Colossians 3:23).

If you're thinking, *Yeah, but you don't understand my situation, how long my hours are, how unappreciated I am, how inconsiderate my boss is, or how toxic my co-workers can be,* I hear you. I've had a lot of jobs throughout my life.

Before I was legally old enough to work, my mom helped me secure a job at the Russian restaurant where her boyfriend worked as a cook. My task? Handing out restaurant flyers for five bucks an hour. My next gig came a bit sneakily—I lied about my age on a job application to snag a position at Pizza Hut, claiming I was sixteen when I was really just fifteen (not my best moment). As I mentioned before, I later worked as a janitor at my church and a leader at the YMCA.

In college, when I landed a job as a recording engineer at an after-school music program, it was the first time I felt genuinely passionate about my work. However, just as I was settling into this role, the 2008 recession hit, and my weekly hours were slashed from thirty-five to fifteen. To make ends meet, I took on additional responsibilities within the program that felt way less exciting. Eventually, I took a position working with adults with developmental disabilities—a job that, while incredibly fulfilling, still wasn't my passion.

My final job before fully committing to my current path was at a church I was attending called The Movement. This role combined all my skills: music, video production, and even public speaking. It catalyzed the launch of my YouTube channel, effectively turning my myriad experiences into a cohesive platform for my passions.

Here's the point: None of these roles was my dream job, yet each one taught me valuable skills I needed later. I'm thankful for all these experiences because they allowed me to sustain myself while dreaming about other things. My friend Curtis King once pointed out that every job is an angel investor—a way to provide financial cover while pursuing passion projects on the side. Just make sure to be aboveboard by giving 100 percent at work. If you're not faithful in the things you *don't* want to do, don't assume you'll be able to muster the discipline to do the things you *are* passionate about later. Habits have a way of following us, so form good ones now.

Wherever you currently are in your journey—whether

you're juggling school classes, homework, and a job; experimenting with a side hustle; discerning your career path; enduring the grind of a nine-to-five; or feeling established several years into your dream job—the daily decision to show up and work hard is not in vain. You are building resilience, grit, and tenacity. God is using this season to prepare you for what's next. He's teaching you invaluable lessons.

If you're able to work to eat, give thanks. Stick with it. Be fully present. Settle in.

SOW TO REAP

While working to eat is about immediate responsibilities—earning enough to sustain you or your family—sowing to reap is about planting seeds for future harvests. This includes working hard in your current role, even when you'd rather be somewhere else. But it also means investing in activities and skills that might not yield immediate benefits but will create long-term success and stability.

This takes incredible patience. The other day, while my kids and I were eating cherries in our backyard, my son suggested planting a cherry seed. Curious, we looked up how long it takes for a cherry tree to mature and bear fruit and were shocked to learn it takes *seven to ten years*. So many things in life work like this: We plant early on, wait patiently, then reap the benefits way later—when we need them most.

Think about this: God knows every hair on your head and every day of your life (Matthew 10:30; Psalm 139:16). He knows exactly when seeds should be planted so you can harvest them at the perfect time. As you follow his lead, he will help you plant at the right moment. At times, it may feel silly to plant seeds—they look so tiny, unimpressive, and inactive. It takes faith to sow. But trust God in this process. As you prayerfully plant, he will bring those seeds to fruition in his timing.

Just as planting a seed today won't yield fruit tomorrow, many of our efforts in life need time to mature. I'm convinced that the main reason people fail at things is due not to a lack of skill but to a lack of perseverance. We plant seeds, water them for a few months, then get impatient and abandon them. Scripture says, "Remember this: Whoever sows sparingly will also reap sparingly, and whoever sows generously will also reap generously" (2 Corinthians 9:6). This verse not only encourages generosity but also calls us to audacity. Have the courage and patience to plant seeds today that, in God's timing, will bear fruit months or years from now.

Here's what sowing has looked like in my journey. After my initial release as an artist, it took four long years to see financial returns from my music. It took another four years before I made a comfortable living, and even then, I didn't quit my day job until 2015. After more than a decade of personal and professional investment, music finally became my sole profession.

Recognizing that music wouldn't occupy all my time, I launched new creative ventures, including my YouTube channel. On my first day as a full-time rapper in 2015, I released a vlog titled "My Day as a Full-Time Rapper." I was planting seeds. Sowing for future seasons. I balanced my time between music and YouTube until I transitioned to focusing solely on YouTube in 2020. By November of that year, YouTube finally became a sustainable income source for my family.

My pattern of sowing to reap has increasingly shortened with each new venture. Whereas music took a decade to bear fruit, YouTube took half that time. My goal to land a book deal took two years to accomplish. Looking back, I can say every moment of waiting was worth it. Even now, I'm planting seeds, trusting God to bring the necessary growth.

So, what seeds can you plant in this season? How is God calling you to trust him with the seeds you've already planted? How can you sow to reap?

DON'T SKIP THE FUNDAMENTALS

If there's one lesson I've learned through years of slogging through mundane jobs and dashed dreams, it's this: *Don't skip the fundamentals; master them.* Every opportunity—even ones you're not excited about—instills certain skills or knowledge in you. It might be the simple discipline of waking up early and getting to work on time. Or perhaps it's developing the humility to take direction from a supervisor (whether they're a great or terrible leader). It might be learning to administrate, organize information, learn software, or manage others. Whether it's mopping the floor or managing a trust fund, take your job seriously. Don't treat any task as beneath you. Remember, Jesus came "not to be served but to serve" (Matthew 20:28, ESV). View your work as a primary way to love your neighbor.

The story of David and Goliath is one of the most famous in the Bible. It's a classic underdog story: A young shepherd takes down a mighty warrior (1 Samuel 17). We admire David's ability to trust God and stand up to his enemies, as we should. But tucked away in this narrative is a lesson about mastering fundamentals.

David's victory didn't start on the battlefield that day. His training wasn't on the front lines of Saul's army. Instead, David's preparation happened in the Judean hills as he tended his father's sheep. It was there, alone in the wilderness, he learned to trust God when wild animals threatened his father's flock. It would have been easy to sacrifice one sheep rather than risk his life facing down a lion, but David chose to fight these smaller battles. He was faithful, even when no one was looking.

When Saul is skeptical of David's offer to fight Goliath, he responds,

> Your servant has been keeping his father's sheep. When a lion or a bear came and carried off a sheep from the flock, I went after it, struck it and rescued the sheep from its mouth. When it turned on me, I seized it by its hair, struck it and killed it. Your servant has killed both the lion and the bear; this uncircumcised Philistine will be like one of them, because he has defied the armies of the living God. The LORD who rescued me from the paw of the lion and the paw of the bear will rescue me from the hand of this Philistine. (1 Samuel 17:34–37)

In this scripture, David offers a compelling example of what it looks like to master the fundamentals. As the youngest son in his family, he tended his father's sheep—a nonglamorous role that wasn't the typical prerequisite for kingship. But David was faithful in the small things: guiding and counting the flock, fending off predators, sleeping in the wilderness, enduring hours of solitude with nothing but sheep for company. How easy it would have been to resent his lowly role. Yet he endured. He did his job with all his strength.

As a result, when David heard Goliath taunting Israel's army, he was fully equipped to bring the giant down. If he hadn't invested the time to learn the fundamentals, he wouldn't have been primed for this moment. Who knows how many hours David practiced with his sling to pass the time while watching his sheep—not to mention the times he actually used it to ward off predators. Due to his preparation, when a high-stakes moment came, he was ready to follow God's lead and save his people.

God "chose David his servant and took him from the sheep pens; from tending the sheep he brought him to be the shepherd of his people Jacob, of Israel his inheritance. And David shepherded them with integrity of heart; with skillful hands he led them" (Psalm 78:70–72).

I love that phrase: *skillful hands*. Every time you're faithful in the little things, God works more skill into your muscle memory. Your hands grow steadier. More confident. Effective.

It's important to recognize that in the narrative about Goliath, David's victory foreshadows the ultimate victory of Jesus. Rather than being Davids ourselves, we're like the scared warriors on the sidelines, fearful of facing the giants in our lives. However, we can draw lessons from David's example of faithfulness. This perspective prevents us from misapplying the story. It helps us understand that while we aren't our own saviors, we can still learn from David's actions and apply those lessons to our lives.

Today's tedium is tomorrow's triumph.

WHAT'S IN YOUR HAND?

The story of David and Goliath also teaches us the value of using what's already in our hands to prepare for future opportunities. Much like David wielded his familiar slingshot and

Moses used his staff, God often uses the ordinary to achieve the extraordinary. For instance, when I first came to faith, I continued making music because rapping was the skill I'd worked hard to cultivate. In many ways, it was one of the few talents I had at the time.

Similarly, David's shepherding was not just a mundane task but a preparation for his eventual kingship. Your current role, no matter how modest it seems, is preparing you for greater responsibility and opportunity. David was called to watch sheep in the fields—what is God calling *you* to right now? How can your present assignment equip you for future roles God might have planned for you?

Whether you're working entry-level jobs, feeling underutilized, or temporarily stepping back from career goals to raise kids or care for a loved one, remember that these seasons of life are not just pauses but preparations. What seems routine is actually foundational. It's building your resilience and readiness for future opportunities.

"The crucible for silver and the furnace for gold, but the LORD tests the heart" (Proverbs 17:3). God refines us because he loves us. He makes us wait to get us ready. He purifies our hearts day by day. Just as gold must be refined to shine brightly, your skills and character must be held to the fire. Every challenge and mundane task is an opportunity to grow and prepare for what lies ahead. Piece by piece, you're becoming who God has called you to be.

When you commit to learning the fundamentals, suddenly ordinary tasks become extraordinary. I'm not an antique collector, but it's fascinating to watch people bring their old "junk" to be appraised by experts on *Antiques Roadshow*. In five minutes, an old trinket bound for the trash becomes treasure—

sometimes worth thousands. Collectors often don't realize the value of what's in their hands. And neither do we.

David wasn't just tending sheep. He was preparing for the throne.

Moses didn't just have a walking stick. He was preparing for Egypt.

You are not just working a job. You are cultivating skills and knowledge you can use for God's kingdom. The work in your hands, which God has given you, is valuable. Don't believe the lie that your work doesn't matter. Even if no one else sees your integrity, hard work, or patience, God does. And he will honor every minute you devote to the fundamentals.

Something striking about David's story is how much of his preparation happened in obscurity, while he humbly tended the flock. No one saw him rescue his sheep from the lion or bear. No one patted him on the back after another sleepless night in the cold. No one awarded him employee of the month.

Likewise, a lot of your best work will go unnoticed and uncelebrated. You may never get a bonus or accolade, even when you go the extra mile. This can be hard to swallow, especially in our social media world where the goal is to be seen, followed, and liked. But God cares more about deepening your character than about building your brand. Unseen work is God's gift to you.

FOCUS ON THE FUNDAMENTALS

We've covered a lot of ground in this chapter, so I want to leave you with a practical takeaway: Identify three or four fundamentals you're learning in your current role. Maybe you've never thought to consider this, and if so, *wonderful*. This will be a new opportunity to look for God's grace in the grind. Whether you work for a paycheck, parent full-time, care for a sick loved one, or [fill in the blank with whatever you give most of your time to], what key skills or character traits is God building in you right now? Those are your fundamentals. I encourage you to write them down and look at them often. To remind yourself that God is working through your current circumstances.

For instance, if you're a dishwasher at a restaurant, maybe God is teaching you to embrace your work with tenacity and integrity. If you're a full-time parent, you might recognize that God is teaching you how to serve with your whole heart and giving you perseverance. If you're a CEO, perhaps God is giving you the skills to lead others well and to make decisions that benefit others. If you're a teacher, God may be showing you how to encourage every student—even the ones who drive you crazy. Perhaps he's helping you reflect his compassionate mercy and love even when it's difficult. If you're starting a business, you might understand that God is teaching you to manage money well and helping you steward your resources wisely.

Whatever your role, take a moment and write down those fundamentals. There is power in naming them. The more you're aware of how God is shaping you, the more motivated you'll be to maximize this season. The skill and knowledge you're gaining in this season will not be wasted.

Don't try to bypass the season you're in. God sees your faithfulness in the little things. Master the fundamentals.

5

Stack Your Talents

Scott Adams, the artist behind the Dilbert comic series, once gave advice that can transform the way we view our creative or vocational work.

In a blog post, he outlined two paths to becoming extraordinary: "become the best at one specific thing" or "become very good (top 25%) at two or more things." Adams argued that the latter path is more attainable for most people. He explained, "Few people will ever play in the NBA or make a platinum record. I don't recommend anyone even try."[1]

Adams's point hits home. When I was young, I devoted myself entirely to basketball, dreaming of a professional career. Reality hit in my sophomore year when I was cut from the junior varsity team. Meanwhile, LeBron James graduated that year and was already a national sensation. In the end, the adage "You can do anything" isn't true. Sometimes people are exponentially better than you. And that's okay.

In our social media world, we have endless exposure to others' talents. Scrolling through your feed can be discouraging. It sometimes feels like *everyone* is moving and shaking their way to the top while you're stuck at the bottom. As a content creator, I have to be very intentional about staying focused on what God has called me to do. If I'm not careful, I'll start comparing myself to others whom I deem more talented or who have more followers. But this is so unproductive.

Rather than beating yourself up about all the people who are better than you, you can *diversify* your skills, which is what Adams calls "building a Talent Stack."[2]

YOU DON'T HAVE TO BE THE BEST

Right now, I want to free you from the pressure to be the best. Few of us will ever achieve that in any skill or vocation. Comparison leads to self-criticism. As you assess your passion, mission, and vocation, opportunities might feel scarce. You might have a passion and sense of mission for something but feel unequipped to pursue it. Perhaps you lack the skills needed, or you feel less than because of how many people are ahead of you. It may seem like everyone else is lapping you while you move at tortoise speed. I've been there many times. As a case in point, when I first started posting videos on YouTube, I had a lot of passion, but the production wasn't great. Still, it was a starting point, and I'll never regret those years of diligent work and constant revision.

That's why Adams's second strategy—to combine two or three talents—is so helpful. It removes the pressure to be the best, which isn't a realistic goal for most of us. Adams wrote, "Everyone has at least a few areas in which they could be in the top 25% with some effort. In my case, I can draw better than most people, but I'm hardly an artist. And I'm not any funnier than the average standup comedian who never makes it big, but I'm funnier than most people. The magic is that few people can draw well and write jokes. It's the combination of the two that makes what I do so rare. And when you add in my business background, suddenly I had a topic that few cartoonists could hope to understand without living it."[3]

Adams concluded with this hint: "You make yourself rare by combining two or more 'pretty goods' until no one else has your mix."[4] By creating your own unique blend of abilities, you can set yourself apart. Turns out, when you combine a few "pretty goods," you get something *very* good. This is talent stacking.

As an indie rapper, skill stacking has been integral to my story. I took my first steps into the music industry by experimenting with freestyle rap. I learned how to use rhythm, cadence, and a robust vocabulary to spontaneously create lyrics. Encouraged by friends, I transitioned from casual freestyling to writing structured songs. My first track, "The Magnificent Lyricist" (epic title, right?), debuted at a local talent show. It was my first real performance, and I loved it.

During my sophomore year of high school, I bought my first computer and began learning music production. With no one to guide me, I taught myself to record and produce tracks. I also shot my own music videos and learned how to use editing software—a skill I didn't have previously. Years later, I took a role at my church managing the live stream operations. This job amalgamated all my skills—including music, video, and public speaking—and catalyzed the launch of my YouTube channel.

In my early days, I primarily saw myself as a creative, focused on the art of music without giving much thought to the business aspect of the industry. However, I quickly realized that to sustain my family and turn my passion into a livelihood, I needed to develop entrepreneurial skills—that is, the ability to transform creativity into a valuable service or product.

The transformation began when my friend Teejay introduced me to a pivotal resource: the *Indie Bible,* a comprehensive guide to building a music career in the mid-2000s. This book not only highlighted my skill deficits but also reshaped my understanding of what it meant to be a successful musician. It taught me that making music wasn't just about art; it was about strategically creating value that could generate profit.

After acknowledging this gap in my skills, I dove headfirst into learning about entrepreneurship. I absorbed insights from thought leaders like John Maxwell, Dave Ramsey, Gary Vaynerchuk, and Michael Hyatt, eventually launching my music label.

Now, more than fifteen years later, I fully identify as an entrepreneur. This journey taught me how to view artistic endeavors through a business lens. I've learned to count the cost before diving into projects, and I'm immensely grateful for the role Teejay and those early resources played in sparking this shift. Thanks to them, art became a way to provide for my family—not just a hobby.

All of this involved skill stacking over the course of decades. My father is an entrepreneur, so perhaps some of the initial spark was genetic. Maybe Teejay saw something in me that I hadn't yet recognized. But ultimately, I had to work diligently to develop these gifts.

In many ways, my career allows me to combine all the skills I've accumulated over a lifetime. Like Adams said, I don't have to be the world's best rapper, video producer, or speaker, though naturally I strive to be excellent in those areas. My success has come from *combining* those abilities in a unique way. That's where the magic happens. And it's the same for you.

WHAT'S YOUR FORMULA?

Think about the skills you possess. How do they make you more valuable in your current role or within your community? By combining them, you can create a unicorn skill set that makes you exceptionally valuable and hard to replace. The aim is to continuously build on your existing skills, layering new ones on top, to forge a unique value proposition that renders you indispensable.

For example, my work combines my love for rap and hip-hop, video production, and cultural commentary from a Christian perspective. There are gifted people in all those spaces, but very few are doing those things simultaneously. As I've followed God's lead and worked hard to acquire these abilities, I've developed my own one-of-a-kind formula.

So, what's your formula? What skills can you combine to offer the world something totally unique? Maybe you've been focused on a particular aptitude, but this conversation is expanding your horizons to see how you can add other gifts to the mix. If you're a teacher with a gift for music or software engineering, find a way to share those talents with your students. If you're a pastor who loves old black-and-white films, find ways to incorporate clips into your sermons. If you work a desk job but love working out, launch a weekly workout club and invite your co-workers. If you have extensive knowledge about Star Wars Lego sets, start making review videos or writing a newsletter or blog.

It sounds cliché, but there is no one like you. Your unique, combined skills and interests are a blessing to the world. Let this be a light bulb moment when different aspects of your life start coming together. Find the threads, and weave them together. Stack your talents.

ACQUIRING NEW SKILLS

Inevitably, as you explore your gifts, you'll discover gaps in your knowledge or ability and new skills you want to acquire. Here's the key question to ask: *What skill, when added to my current tool belt, will exponentially increase my value offering?* Please hear me: I'm not saying your value as a person hinges on your marketability. Far from it—you are created and loved by God, regardless of how talented or wealthy you are. God's love for you doesn't depend on your résumé. That said, God graciously invites us to broaden our skill sets so we can both provide for ourselves personally *and* bless others. To bring *others* value for *his* glory, as well as for our benefit.

As much as I love rapping, it was hard to make a living from it. Yet when I combined my knack for business, video production (YouTube), and cultural commentary, I finally hit my stride.

Which new skill would take what you do to the next level?

For example, if you're organized, comfortable using a computer, and good with numbers, consider learning accounting software like QuickBooks. Launch a side hustle offering bookkeeping services to small business owners.

If you have an eye for graphic design, take a class to learn Adobe Photoshop or Illustrator. Knowing how to use industry-standard tools will make you even more marketable. It's crazy to me how many talented people skip steps like this, because they're intimidated by unknown software or don't want to make time to learn it. Invest the time and reap the benefits.

Maybe you love making things with your hands—sewing, woodworking, or crafting, for example. You'd like to sell what you make, but you're not sure how to launch an online business. Learning e-commerce, on sites like Amazon or Etsy, might be your next step.

If you're always fixing things around the house, or helping friends with building projects, why not get your contractor's license? Or launch a furniture-building or repair business? Yes, it's a bit of work, but once you've started, you'll generate extra income.

Skill stacking is innovative: It works with what you have and makes it better. It starts where you are and helps you reach new heights. The point is, you already have momentum in what you're doing. Now it's time to add fuel to the fire. If you feel burned out or bored with your current job, resist the temptation to slip into autopilot. Brainstorm what it would look like to add new skills to your tool belt.

If you're in a busy season, juggling many responsibilities, you're probably thinking, *I don't have time to add something extra to my plate. Are you crazy?*

Trust me, I hear you. The good news is, people have researched how long it takes to grow proficient in a new skill. In many cases, it's not as involved as you think. Experts tell us that, surprisingly, you don't need a ton of time to learn a new skill—you just need twenty hours.

ALL YOU NEED IS TWENTY HOURS

Adding new skills can be challenging. It demands dedication and a willingness to step into the unknown, often without immediate recognition or encouragement. In Josh Kaufman's book, *The First 20 Hours,* he makes a striking claim: With twenty hours of dedicated, focused practice, you can become proficient in nearly any skill.[5] For instance, you can learn to play basic chords on a guitar or piano. Or learn the basics of a software application. Or learn to bake artisan bread. Or master the fundamentals of pickleball.

Typically, we don't set time limits when learning something new. As a result, when it gets difficult, we give up. The twenty-hour rule provides a helpful milestone—something to aim for. You'll be surprised by what you can accomplish in this limited time frame.

In the summer of 2023, I recognized the need to diversify my business beyond the unreliable algorithm of Google's AdSense (a program that allows creators to earn money by displaying ads on their websites and YouTube videos). So, I tackled a new skill—developing and merchandising products for my audience. I learned tools like Canva, Photoshop, and Illustrator and built relationships with manufacturers overseas.

Balancing this with an already busy schedule was challenging, but I carved out thirty to sixty minutes every night to research and refine designs, often after my family was asleep. When I hit creative or logistical walls, it was frustrating, but persistence paid off. Learning this skill revolutionized my business, decreasing my financial reliance on YouTube from 90 percent to 25 percent. Merchandise and other products like prayer journals became the majority of my income. Not only did this provide a stabler revenue stream, but it also freed me to serve my audience better by offering value instead of chasing the algorithm.

Your Next Step

Acquiring new skills isn't easy. You'll have to step out of your comfort zone. For some, the hardest part is getting started, while others experience the midway slump. Yet with a bit of grit and perseverance, you will grow exponentially. By committing to this path, you're setting the stage for substantial personal and professional growth that will make you an invaluable asset wherever you choose to apply your talents.

Reflect on your existing skills. What unique combination of abilities can you offer the world? Remember, you don't have to be the best at one thing—just above average in a few things. Start there, then reflect on a new skill you want to cultivate. Decide what your next step is, whether it's enrolling in a digital course, watching tutorials, finding a mentor, or applying for a business license.

Now, here's the most important part. Good intentions won't accomplish anything. If you're serious about building new skills and stacking them, you need a specific plan. You need to know *when* and *where* and *for how long* you will practice.

For example, if your goal is to learn basic guitar chords, your plan could look like this:

> **When:** On Monday, Wednesday, and Friday mornings
> **Where:** In my living room
> **For how long:** Thirty minutes

If your goal is to learn Pro Tools (music recording software), you might set this plan:

When: Monday through Friday at 7 p.m.
Where: In my home office
For how long: Twenty minutes

Put it on your calendar, and give yourself twenty hours over the next few months to go after it. With consistent effort—even fifteen minutes a day—your investment will compound over time. You'll be amazed by how much you can accomplish.

The goal is to gradually expand your abilities, one step at a time. As your skill stack grows, your opportunities will too.

6

Follow the Favor

I've always been fascinated by the backstories of famous products—especially those that were originally intended for a completely different purpose. Here are a few examples:

- Coca-Cola started out as a cure for the inventor's morphine addiction.
- Listerine was originally used as an antiseptic.
- Bubble Wrap was intended to be a new style of wallpaper.
- The Slinky was invented to help stabilize naval equipment on rough seas.
- Rogaine was intended to treat high blood pressure.
- Chain saws were developed to cut bones during operations.
- WD-40 was created for lubricating missiles.
- Play-Doh was first invented to clean sooty walls.[1]

The creator of each of these products likely had a moment of surprise when their research, preparation, and testing took them in an unforeseen direction. Suddenly, a market they didn't anticipate revealed itself. These inventors could have dug their heels in, refusing to surrender their initial visions. To their credit, they leaned in, recognizing that every dream is pliable. Instead of a closed door, they each saw a new opportunity.

What's the lesson? As you discern your calling, don't be surprised if God leads you into unexpected territory. The skills you develop, the business you start, or the degree you earn *might* take you to your expected destination, but it's possible you'll end up somewhere entirely unexpected. Keep your wits about you. Listen for God's voice. What looks like a detour might be God's leading.

It's human nature to want certainty. Once we set our course, we're reluctant to deviate. We'll even say things like "God told me to go *this* way"—which may be true, but God has a knack for rerouting us according to his wisdom. To be called by God makes you *more* adaptable, not less. Think of David, who seemed content to be a shepherd, *until* he was anointed as king. Or Saul in the New Testament, whose plan A was to persecute Christians into extinction, *until* Christ met him on the road to Damascus. Or Peter, who planned to make a living as a fisherman, *until* he hauled in a net full of fish at Christ's command.

I want to free you from the burden of knowing "God's only calling" for your life. God doesn't force you into a straitjacket; he's placed you in a garden where you can explore, try new things, and find your focus. It's a process, not a formula.

MY ZIGZAG JOURNEY

Initially, my contributions to YouTube were centered on music. I gave advice to other rappers, which eventually led me to create a Patreon where artists could pay for music reviews. The community grew into a stable revenue stream, and while YouTube wasn't generating much income for me at that point, my Patreon took off.

As the music review sessions gained momentum, my audience began steering the conversation toward broader cultural topics and events. At first, the questions were rooted in the music industry: What did I think of certain trends or shifts in the landscape? But soon, those questions began to shift. People wanted to hear my take on larger cultural issues. They wanted to know more about my personal values and faith. Initially, I was hesitant to bring my faith into these discussions. I wanted to keep the focus on music and avoid venturing into territory that could potentially alienate a portion of my audience. But the more my community kept asking for it, the more I obliged. They'd ask questions like these:

"What do you think about this event?"

"What would you do in this situation?"

"What do Christians believe about that?"

It became clear they were looking for more than music advice. This was a pivotal moment. I realized there was a demand for these kinds of conversations, and rather than shy away from them, I leaned in. To dip my toe into the water, I began experimenting by clipping sections of these discussions and sharing them more broadly. The response was positive, showing me that the hunger for more faith-based, culturally relevant content was real. My YouTube channel evolved in ways I never anticipated, and I'm *so thankful* it did.

How do you discern what God is calling you to focus on in this season? It's a great question—one I've asked incessantly throughout my career. Here are a few thoughts to guide you.

HOLD YOUR IDEAS LOOSELY

In a world of filtered photos and highlight reels, success is made to look easy. But the journey from point A to point B is seldom linear. It's always full of twists and turns, which means you must hold your ideas loosely. Don't get so married to your method that you drive yourself mad. If you're inflexible, change will break you. But if you're malleable, change will unleash your potential. Your first idea is rarely your best idea, as James Clear writes: "Inspiration comes on the twenty-fifth attempt, not the first. If you want to make something excellent, don't wait for a brilliant idea to strike. Create twenty-five of what you need and one will be great. Inspiration reveals itself after you get the average ideas out of the way, not before you take the first step."[2]

Things almost never turn out exactly how you planned, and that's okay. In fact, Scripture encourages us to make tentative plans, entrusting the final results to God. "Now listen, you who say, 'Today or tomorrow we will go to this or that city, spend a year there, carry on business and make money.' Why, you do not even know what will happen tomorrow. What is your life? You are a mist that appears for a little while and then vanishes. Instead, you ought to say, 'If it is the Lord's will, we will live and do this or that'" (James 4:13–15).

To modern ears, this may sound restricting. Popular wisdom tells us that we determine our own destinies—that we can do and be whatever we want. But as Christians, we know we're *not* in control, and that's wonderful news. Our time here is short, so why not partner with God and follow his lead? In our pursuit of excellence, even if we fail, God is still on his throne and we are still dearly loved.

When you sense he's leading you in a new direction, don't hesitate to follow. None of the skills you've developed will be wasted or forgotten; they'll simply be used in fresh ways. Hold your ideas loosely. God's got you.

GET FEEDBACK EARLY AND OFTEN

Two years ago, the format of my content was primarily talking-head videos with a catchy intro to capture attention. We had built up an audience, so I asked them for feedback (something I encourage every creator or entrepreneur to do). Once people are paying attention, their feedback becomes the catalyst for innovation.

I love looking for up-and-coming creators, which led me to connect with Tim Ross, who invited me onto his podcast. I flew myself out to his town, and we had a fantastic two-hour conversation. His podcast, *The Basement with Tim Ross,* exploded after our episode and a few others—eventually becoming a popular podcast on Apple. What made that experience eye-opening was the feedback I received from my own audience. Many hadn't seen me in a long-form podcast setting in a while, and their response made me realize I needed to reintroduce that format.

So at the end of 2022, we relaunched our own podcast. This move doubled our Patreon community and provided a fresh revenue stream that stabilized our business. What began as a single podcast appearance led to the rediscovery of my passion for interviewing. Now a significant part of my platform is built on those long-form conversational podcasts, attracting guests like *New York Times* bestselling authors and well-known musicians. It's a perfect example of how listening to feedback can shift your trajectory.

Yet sometimes feedback creates confusion before it yields clarity. When I began shifting my focus from music reviews to cultural topics, part of my audience wasn't entirely on board. They'd drop comments in the chat, encouraging me to stick to the music and avoid straying too far into social commentary. It caught me off guard at first, and internally, I felt that tension too. Until then, I had avoided trending topics. There was a constant tug-of-war in my mind: Was I saying too much or too little? Should I delve into these issues more deeply, or was I dividing my audience? It was a delicate balance, but ultimately, through trial and error and by listening closely to my community, I found a sweet spot. Over time, my work became more focused.

As you strive to focus your efforts, consider who can best provide feedback. It may be customers instead of a social media audience. It may be your first client or two. It could even be your friends and family. Listen to those trusted voices who are invested in who you are and what you do. Their advice will sharpen your vision.

MAKE INCREMENTAL ADJUSTMENTS

Once you've captured feedback, it's time to improve. A slogan I created is "Incremental adjustments lead to monumental advancements." Here are some examples of what I mean:

If you carve out a few hours each week to meal prep, you'll save a substantial amount of money by not wasting food or eating out, you'll avoid empty calories by eating more nutritious foods, and you'll eliminate decision fatigue from having to figure out what to eat every day. It's one small investment that yields healthy results.

In terms of spiritual health, when you invest time in your relationship with God—through prayer, Scripture, and community—you feel closer to him and develop a more serious practice of your faith.

Financially, if you commit time each month to budgeting and tracking expenses, even using simple tools like an envelope system, you can make serious progress toward getting out of debt.

All these seemingly small investments compound over time, leading to monumental advancements in every area of life.

Many people don't realize that incremental investments can completely revolutionize their lives. Again, small intentional actions in specific areas can lead to monumental changes. But there's a catch—taking on too much too fast can lead to burnout and overwhelm, causing us to do nothing at all. That's why it's crucial to identify where to start. What's the one small investment that can spark a domino effect and cause the rest to fall into place?

If you want to create lasting change, making tiny adjustments over a long period of time has several advantages. First, too much change, too fast, will tire you out and create confusion. Better to go at a slower pace you can maintain. Second, you often won't know whether a change is positive or negative until you try it. By implementing change in small doses, you can continue to adjust along the way, thus avoiding bigger mistakes. Third, small changes are more sustainable. And *powerful*. Over time, one small change can have a massive impact. James Clear provides a helpful illustration:

> Imagine you are flying from Los Angeles to New York City. If a pilot leaving from LAX adjusts the

> heading just 3.5 degrees south, you will land in Washington, D.C., instead of New York. Such a small change is barely noticeable at takeoff—the nose of the airplane just moves a few feet—but when magnified across the entire United States, you end up hundreds of miles apart.[3]

The power of tiny changes has altered the course of my career. In the early days, innovation for me came in the form of technology. In 2018, using a video switcher to live stream with multiple camera angles was rare in the YouTube space. It set my content apart. As I continued to evolve, my next big shift was recognizing the success of covering trending topics and offering cultural commentary.

By the end of 2020, I was working seven days a week and knew I couldn't keep carrying the load alone. The best decision I made was hiring my COO, Zach Sperrazzo. Zach not only helped alleviate the pressure on me but also played a huge role in helping me innovate further. With his support, we moved beyond relying solely on live streams. He encouraged us to script out more-polished edited videos, optimize thumbnails, and improve overall packaging. Zach helped me shift from a reactive, spur-of-the-moment style to a more intentional content strategy.

From there, I continued to make incremental investments in my team. We brought on Chris to handle editing and then Semaj to refine our thumbnails. As we constantly reinvested and improved the operation, the quality of our content skyrocketed. The content I'm creating now is on a completely different level compared to what I was doing in 2020. Each small investment made a huge difference—whether it was better lighting, more thoughtful guests, or a format revamp.

The key lesson here is that innovation isn't something you do once and stop; it's a continuous process. There's always room for improvement. Think about your workspace, technology use, and workflow, as well as how people relate to your work. What is one small way you can improve what you do?

DOUBLE DOWN ON YOUR WINS

As you experiment with incremental changes, be on the lookout for signs of life. Where are these changes having a positive impact? For me, my transition to cultural commentary (though it turned off some viewers) ultimately attracted *way* more people to my platform. It happened gradually, but once I noticed the positive pattern, I poured more time and resources into producing that kind of content. A friend of mine says, "Go where the favor is." In other words, pay attention to where your hard work is paying off. Where do you see God's blessing? Where do you naturally have favor with others? Invest in those areas.

Be wary of moving on too soon from an implemented change. Like a seed lying dormant beneath the soil, some of your most productive changes will take time to mature. If you rush from one shiny new idea to another, you'll be too distracted to notice if one sprouts. When you find one of those little green shoots, tend it. Nurture it. See how big it will grow.

Attentive gardeners don't just scatter seed at random, nor do they water plants without careful consideration. In the same way, take the time to monitor every change you make.

If you're trying to grow your social media platform, track your followers. Notice which posts garner the most attention, then ask why.

If your co-workers regularly come to you for advice on a particular topic, how can you reach more people with your advice or knowledge?

If you're selling out of one product but barely breaking even on another, put all your effort into the one that's succeeding.

If something in you comes alive every time you teach the Bible, how can you do more of that? Who in your circle would benefit from it?

If you share your business idea with friends, watch their faces closely to see when their eyes light up and when they seem bored. Ask questions about what does and doesn't matter to them.

Look for signs of life. Double down on your wins.

FOLLOW GOD'S LEAD

Life throws curveballs, but it's often these disruptions that produce some of our best ideas. If you commit to the process, making small changes over the long haul, your calling will grow clearer in your mind and heart. It's a wonderful adventure to partner with God—to let him guide you into uncharted territory. With open hands, follow his lead.

As you do, your number one obstacle will be distraction. And I don't just mean the phone-scrolling, Netflix-streaming type. Many distractions come disguised in "productive" packages.

In the next chapter, we'll learn how to detect and defeat distraction in all its forms so you can stay focused on the good work God is calling you to do.

7

Defeat Distraction

I'm in my studio, looking for content ideas. I see the usual suspects—a church leader embroiled in controversy, a heated debate between two theologians, the latest alien theory circulating on social media.

But it doesn't stop there. I get pulled into a tech review, curious about some gadget I don't really need. A new music release catches my eye, so naturally, I give it a listen. The tabs on my internet browser multiply: a random documentary, a trending X thread, a video essay about the decline of civilization. I tell myself I'm being productive, staying informed, but the reality is, I'm not actually accomplishing anything.

Can you relate?

It's the moment you look up from your phone after scrolling on social media, only to realize an hour has gone by. It's the dissatisfaction of a to-do list that sits untouched because you can't focus. It's the underlying sense of failure because your actions don't align with your goals.

The predominant thing standing in your way isn't your ability—it's distraction. For so many (myself included), it's a struggle to stay focused. While on tour as a rapper, I learned firsthand the folly of trying to juggle selling merch, performing, driving, scheduling, and doing interviews—not to mention loving my family well and staying connected to Jesus. It wore me down. Maybe you're feeling depleted in this season. Your attention is split in a thousand directions. You're not sure how to hone in on your goals because life seems to pull you away.

Distraction isn't always laziness. Sometimes it's a coping mechanism when we've taken on more than we can handle. On any given day, you have a finite amount of willpower. Despite the cultural maxim that you can "do anything you put your mind to," God has given you limits. And this is for your good. The world doesn't depend on you, which means you can rest, trusting in his power and goodness to carry you. The paradox between knowing your limits and being productive is heavily influenced by our environment and feeling replenished and refreshed. This is why removing distractions and implementing virtue—like spending time with God—is so essential.

Everything I'm about to say is not meant to pile guilt onto your exhaustion. Sure, you might need to reckon with your proclivity to distraction and work hard to remove those temptations. But more than anything, this chapter is an invitation to a more satisfying, organized, simple way of life. I want to give you the same tools that have helped this frenetic rapper build a six-figure business—something I never dreamed I'd accomplish. By God's grace, I've learned to limit distraction and run hard after my calling.

Here's what most people omit from the conversation about distraction: It's a *spiritual* issue, not just a time-management issue. The way you steward your time and honor your commitments shows what you believe about God and your role in his story. Jesus takes the commitments we make—to him and others—very seriously.

LET YOUR YES BE YES

In our culture, commitments are often casual. We RSVP for a party, but who knows if we'll actually show up? We'd rather select "maybe" and keep our options open than have to be somewhere at a specific time. Even when pursuing passion projects, if the going gets tough, we seek relief in mindless distractions. Rather than forge ahead, we flake out. I've done it. Chances are, you have too.

While we know distraction isn't good, we rarely consider its effects on our souls. At its core, focus is not primarily about efficiency; it's about integrity. It's about following through with what we said we would do. In his famous Sermon on the Mount, Jesus challenges our flimsy oaths and calls us to keep our word:

> You have heard that it was said to the people long ago, "Do not break your oath, but fulfill to the Lord the vows you have made." But I tell you, do not swear an oath at all: either by heaven, for it is God's throne; or by the earth, for it is his footstool; or by Jerusalem, for it is the city of the Great King. And do not swear by your head, for you cannot make even one hair white or black. All you need to say is simply "Yes" or "No"; anything beyond this comes from the evil one. (Matthew 5:33–37)

As God's people, our trademark should be reliability, integrity, and dependability. This goes for our personal lives (the habits we cultivate) as well as our public lives (our relationships).

True, Jesus sets the bar high. While there's plenty of grace when life takes over and prevents us from following through, it's God's *kindness* that calls us to honor our commitments. He invites you into a peaceful and productive existence rather than a life of hurried distraction. A life free from the guilt of unkept promises. A life that's full but still leaves margin to enjoy God, pursue hobbies, take walks, care for your family, and love your neighbors.

If God has called you to something, he will provide the margin to accomplish it. Distraction leaves us scattered and overwhelmed. It frazzles us into thinking we don't have time for the tasks and relationships that matter the most.

So if you desire to go all-in on your God-given assignment in this season, distraction has to go.

This is about more than decluttering your calendar: It's a call to worship. As Paul writes, "I urge you, brothers and sisters, in view of God's mercy, to offer your bodies as a living sacrifice, holy and pleasing to God—this is your true and proper worship" (Romans 12:1).

So, let's kill distraction. Let's worship.

HOW TO DEFEAT DISTRACTION

If you had told me ten years ago that this scatterbrained rapper, who stayed up late and had a knack for midnight doughnut runs, would one day oversee a talented team, run a successful business, and live a disciplined life, I would have laughed. Similarly, you might question whether you have what it takes to weed out distraction from your life.

In this chapter, I'll walk you through six principles that help me focus on my goals. Like anyone, I still get sidetracked more than I care to admit. But I've improved drastically from where I used to be, and if you implement these principles, you'll be surprised by how much more you will enjoy your work.

PRINCIPLE 1:
SET A SPECIFIC LIMIT ON MEDIA CONSUMPTION

Because I'm a content creator on YouTube, it may seem counterintuitive—even hypocritical—for me to recommend less media consumption. Currently, viewers have logged over *seventeen million* watch hours on my channels (and counting). This is staggering. In some ways, my career in media makes me *more* aware of the dangers of distraction, since I work from the belly of the beast. There's no way around it: Modern people are media junkies. We're addicted to glowing screens, endlessly scrolling for something to entertain or inform us. My goal is to provide content that glorifies Jesus and improves people's lives, but I'll be the first to admit that sometimes I worry I'm contributing to the problem.

When was the last time you checked the statistics on how much media Americans consume? In 2020, consumers in the U.S. spent almost *eight hours a day* consuming television, Netflix, and social media.[1] And the number has hovered around seven hours a day every year since 2021.[2] Every time my phone pings me with a screen time report, I wince a bit. *Did I really spend that much time on my phone this week?*

Imagine if you reclaimed half of the national screen time average—four hours a day—to develop skills to move you from where you are to where you want to be. What if you sacrificed some of those eight hours to work on a new side hustle, manage your finances, or invest in a skill or hobby?

I have nothing against Netflix, Instagram, or YouTube, but none of these platforms gives a rip about your goals. They're engineered to hook your attention, which means they're *enemies* of your goals. Streaming is all about immediate reward. A show ends, and before you have time to consider a productive next move, the next episode starts automatically. It's a win for Netflix but a loss for your godly ambition.

Excessive streaming and scrolling distract us from developing the skills and habits that align with our godly ambitions and long-term goals. By consciously choosing to limit our consumption, we can redirect that time and energy toward more productive pursuits. It's an investment in our personal and spiritual growth.

I don't want to be overly prescriptive. There's no magic number for how much time you should spend consuming media each day. The most important thing I recommend is to be *specific*. For example, pledge to limit your media consumption to two nights per week or perhaps one hour each day. Or limit yourself to three podcast episodes a week. Or maybe commit to checking social media only during your lunch break. If your nightly routine is to watch shows or YouTube, set a limit and fill the newfound space with productive or life-giving pursuits—like researching a side hustle, networking, going for a walk, reading on a topic that interests you, going on dates with your spouse, praying, learning a new sport, or gathering with friends.

Initially, cutting back will feel like a painful sacrifice. It's not easy to reshape your routines. However, the short-term sacrifice will yield positive long-term returns. Like a snowball rolling down a hill, your growth will gain a little more momentum with each tiny investment. After a while, you'll start enjoying the feeling of progress. Your mind will relish the margin to dream and solve problems. Your godly ambition will grow stronger as you feed it.

So, where do you need to cut back on media consumption? Make a plan, and honor the commitment you make.

Principle 2:
Create Before Consuming

One of the simplest and most effective principles I live by is to *create before consuming*. Deep-rooted in our souls is the desire to create. In the beginning, when God created the heavens and the earth and, finally, formed the first humans in his image, his first instruction was for them to create. To take the raw materials given to them and reshape them into things that were useful and beautiful: "God blessed them and said to them, 'Be fruitful and increase in number; fill the earth and subdue it. Rule over the fish in the sea and the birds in the sky and over every living creature that moves on the ground'" (Genesis 1:28). We have an innate desire to create because we are made in the image and likeness of God our Creator.

Even simple acts qualify as "creating." For example, my day typically begins with a personal quiet time, when I read the Bible and write in my prayer journal. This act of writing is a form of creation; it involves documenting my requests to God and reflecting on his Word. To start with a small burst of creativity as an act of worship sets a purposeful tone for my day.

Later in the morning, I continue to apply this principle by integrating media consumption with other productive activities. For instance, I might listen to a podcast or watch a video while exercising. When using platforms like Instagram, I contribute before I consume. I maintain a channel where I post daily devotional thoughts based on the chapter of Proverbs I read that day. Similarly, when working on YouTube, I prioritize publishing my own videos daily before scoping out what others are producing.

If you create before you consume, you will be more purposeful and less passive. You'll be someone who contributes to the good of others. Think through your current ratio of creating versus consuming. What is one simple way you can prioritize the former before settling into the latter?

Principle 3:
Choose a Few Daily Non-Negotiables

In *The Power of Habit,* Charles Duhigg explains the power of a "keystone habit"—a consistent behavior or pattern that has a big impact.[3] Once established, a keystone habit triggers a domino effect of positive changes in your life.

For example, if daily exercise is your keystone habit, it will most likely trigger you to begin preparing healthy breakfasts, scheduling regular sleep times, and setting daily workout goals. The keystone habit provides the needed structure to support these smaller habits and keep you on track. Without the keystone habit, your goals would crumble.[4]

Keystone habits are what I call "non-negotiables"—daily actions I do *no matter what*. This is what these patterns look like in my life:

> **Spiritual morning routine:** Every day starts with reading Scripture, focusing on a chapter from Prov-

erbs, and reflecting on a memory verse. This practice, often done outdoors at sunrise, sets a reflective tone for the day and includes writing in my prayer journal about praise, prayers for others, and personal requests.

Physical activity: Regular exercise is integral to my morning, whether it's a neighborhood walk while listening to an audiobook, a workout on the assault bike, or a strength-training session. This physical engagement clears my mind and energizes my body for the day's challenges.

Family time: Prioritizing at least one or two meals with my family daily, usually breakfast and dinner, helps us bond and share our daily experiences. Each evening, we have a "rose and thorn" discussion to talk about the highs and lows of our day. Additionally, I spend time reading Bible stories with my kids and investing in their spiritual growth, not to mention having fun and playing games together.

Evening wind down: The day ends with quality time with my wife, often watching a show or discussing our day. This downtime is vital for reconnecting and unwinding.

I break my professional goals down into non-negotiables as well. For instance, on YouTube, I publish a specific number of videos each week. This objective translates into specific daily tasks: Each day we release one main-channel video, two videos for a second channel, and one clip for my business channel.

To pull this off, my team and I stream four days a week. During these streaming sessions, I keep a clock in front of me to stay focused and on schedule, ensuring that each segment is concise and on topic. Left to my own devices, I'm quite distractible, so a disciplined schedule and clear, actionable goals are essential. By replacing unstructured time with focused, productive activities, I've matured and advanced in my professional and personal life.

How to Follow Through

Setting non-negotiables is one thing. Actually *doing* them is another. In Jon Acuff's book *Quitter,* he debunks the myth that those who flake on commitments lack desire. Instead, he says it's the internal debate between one's reluctant self today and one's motivated self from yesterday. His solution? Anytime you're tempted to give up, tell yourself, "We've already discussed this and made the commitment; this is happening."[5] It's a simple, almost comical step, but I've found it helpful.

Acuff stresses that rehashing "the discussion" is exhausting and that each loss makes the next victory harder. So, decide once, carry it out, and put an end to the internal debate. He calls this approach "death to the discussion," a method to stop self-sabotage and stick to your commitments.

In my case, one of my decisions was to wake up early. For an artist—especially one accustomed to late-night performances and creative sessions—adjusting to an early-morning routine disrupted my creative rhythm. Initially, the struggle to alter my schedule was compounded by the demanding nature and sporadic lifestyle of touring. Sleep deprivation was not uncommon, as nighttime performances and early-morning drives prevented any chance of a regular sleep pattern.

However, the decision to start my day earlier eventually became a pivotal change. This new routine allowed me to establish a consistent morning devotional practice, which not only strengthened my spiritual resilience but also enhanced my physical health and mental clarity. The discipline of rising early provided a sense of purpose, setting a positive tone for the day and enabling more-focused work. These morning hours have become a sanctuary—something I look forward to. It's my time to reflect, prepare, breathe.

Practice saying this to yourself right now so that when a moment of weakness comes, you're ready to go: "We've already discussed this and made the commitment; this is happening."

Don't sabotage your own plans. Stick with your nonnegotiables.

Principle 4:
Optimize Your Environment for Deep Work

I'm a content creator, so my work is fast-paced, technology-driven, and influenced by current events. In other words, my life is a recipe for interruption, distraction, and multitasking. Much like you, I have to think on my feet and pivot in real time, based on in-the-moment trends or opportunities.

That said, I've learned the power of what Cal Newport calls "deep work," which refers to "professional activities performed in a state of distraction-free concentration that push your cognitive capabilities to their limit. These efforts create new value, improve your skill, and are hard to replicate."[6] Having undistracted concentration and pushing yourself to the limit might sound intense if you're just trying to get through the day unscathed. I get it. However, without the ability to concentrate for an extended period, distraction will derail your dreams.

Because I'm a full-time YouTuber, producing music has become increasingly challenging. The process typically starts well—I set aside time to write and record, diving into the creative flow. However, when I pause to look up a Bible verse or a cultural reference to enhance a lyric, I quickly get distracted, spiraling down a rabbit hole of unrelated YouTube videos. I end up frustrated and unproductive.

If you're serious about protecting your time and following through with your goals, deep work is essential. Your mind needs time to focus exclusively on the task at hand. Here are a few tactics I use to enter deep work:

1. **Put your phone aside:** One of my key strategies for achieving deep work is removing my phone from my immediate reach. This simple action reduces interruptions and helps maintain my focus on the task at hand. By minimizing the temptation to check notifications, I can dive deeper into my creative process without external distractions.
2. **Optimize your workspace:** I arrange my studio in a way that supports deep work. For example, I ensure there's plenty of natural light. I keep my desk uncluttered. A clean and bright workspace not only enhances my mood but also improves my ability to concentrate. This environment invites creativity and helps me stay engaged in my work for longer periods.

3. **Adapt your workflow:** I start working on music before my team arrives, usually around 9:30 A.M., to take advantage of the quiet hours. When recording, I don't force myself to complete a verse in a linear fashion; if a line isn't coming to me, I skip it and work on a different part of the song. This flexible approach allows me to keep progressing, even when parts of the project are challenging. If necessary, I shift to another song entirely. This might seem sporadic, but it ensures I'm stewarding my time well.

Principle 5:
Gamify Your Goals

Another strategy for limiting distraction is to make reaching goals more fun. One way I gamify my work is through a bonus structure tied directly to our gross revenue. Humans naturally love numbers, and for my team, knowing the specific revenue we generate each month helps us connect the inputs of our efforts to the outputs we want to achieve. Every month, we set a clear revenue goal as a company, and if we hit that number, every team member receives a bonus on top of their regular salary. This creates a healthy sense of motivation and excitement around reaching targets, and it keeps everyone focused on the tangible results of their work. It's a simple but effective way to reward yourself for staying focused.

Gamifying your goals doesn't have to be complex—start by identifying one area of your work or life where you can create a simple challenge or reward system. For example, if you're trying to stay consistent with a project or habit, set a goal for the number of tasks you complete each day, then track your progress visually, such as through a checklist, a calendar, or a journal. Celebrate when you hit those small milestones. If you're working on a creative project, challenge yourself to complete a specific number of words, designs, or pieces of content, knowing that those inputs will lead to bigger results down the line. The goal is not just to reach the final outcome but also to build momentum by rewarding the consistent effort it takes to get there. Think of one area where you can break down your work into smaller, measurable actions, and make tracking those actions a game that keeps you motivated.

TEND THE GARDEN

We've covered a lot of ground, including limiting media intake, creating before consuming, choosing non-negotiables, and pursuing deep work. In a perfect world, we could implement these principles without a hitch. However, as you know, that's not the world we live in. Don't put pressure on yourself to execute these ideas flawlessly; instead, expect setbacks. Give yourself permission to fail. Work out the kinks. Revise and iterate as needed.

Think of your habits like a garden. You can't just plant seeds and hope all goes well. Every thriving garden must constantly be monitored, especially when it comes to removing weeds. Media consumption and other distractions—what Song of Songs 2:15 calls "little foxes that ruin the vineyards"—seek to derail your growth. If you fail to remove them, they'll take over and healthy habits will get choked out. It's often the small, seemingly insignificant things that cause the greatest harm if left unaddressed.

Here's a quick example: Instagram is a strategic platform for creativity, but it's quite addictive. If I'm not careful, it opens the door for toxic comparison and lust. After recognizing this negative impact, I removed Instagram from my iPhone and now manage my social media interactions through a business iPad. This significantly reduces distractions and, most importantly, helps me safeguard my mental and emotional well-being.

At the end of the day, God cares more about our character than our success. He calls us to prioritize purity over productivity. As a business owner, I know how easy it is to justify using certain tools or platforms because they're "industry standard." We don't want to be at a disadvantage. We want to keep up. But if we ignore weeds in the name of "growth," our lives will end up unhealthy. If you ignore small problems, instead of going away, they'll become *bigger* problems.

Evaluate your habits. Where do you see distraction thriving? Where are you not following through on your goals? Where do you need encouragement, accountability, and inspiration? Where are you faithful, and where are you fumbling? Your life is a garden, and God expects you to care for it well. So, tend the garden.

PUTTING IT ALL TOGETHER

Let's wrap up with a few reflective questions. These are designed to help you process this chapter and take your next steps to defeat distraction.

> **Limiting media consumption:** What is your media plan? Set specific times for consumption, and stick to them to avoid the trap of endless scrolling, which can lead to comparison and discontent.

Creating before consuming: What habit or routine will prevent you from passively overconsuming content and push you toward more creativity and productivity?

Establishing daily non-negotiables: What are simple daily actions that will compound over time and move you closer to your goals? How can you implement these actions every day?

Promoting deep work: How can you optimize your environment for deep work? Consider what changes will make your space less distracting, more inviting, and conducive for focused work.

Tending the garden: Despite your best intentions and systems, where is distraction still a problem? How do you need to revamp or reorder your life to remove the "weeds"?

8

Collaborate with Others

In 2019, while traveling full-time for my music career, I interviewed with various artists and creators, one of whom was BrandMan Sean. I initially connected with him through his YouTube channel, which focused on marketing tactics for rappers. Our relationship continued to grow, and by 2020, just before the pandemic, he visited my studio in California for a discussion on my live stream.

Fast-forward to 2023, when Sean invited me to appear on his new podcast. At this time, my main source of income was AdSense, which, as I mentioned before, involved earning money from ads displayed on my YouTube videos. But YouTube's algorithms are unpredictable—which is unnerving when, besides providing for your family, you employ a team who depends on you.

During Sean's podcast, I shared my idea to develop a custom prayer journal based on my long-standing habit of recording prayers in notebooks. This simple system has had a significant impact on me. Sean immediately recognized the potential of this idea and urged me to act on it. Motivated by his encouragement, I got to work with the help of my COO, Zach, and my wife, Monette. We secured a manufacturer, and by the summer of that year, we launched the Bless God Prayer Journal, which to date has sold over fifteen thousand copies. Afterward, we introduced a leadership planner that integrated features of the prayer journal with additional planning tools. This venture has provided revenue streams beyond AdSense and has transformed our business.

BETTER TOGETHER

You will go much further with others than you will alone. Make networking and relationship building a staple in your life. Without Sean's encouragement, I don't know whether I would have moved forward with the project. Beyond the benefits for my business, I truly believe the prayer journal has blessed people. Many have expressed how it has deepened their walk with Jesus, and for that, I'm grateful.

This is the power of proximity. Especially in our disconnected digital age, we need to be in the same room—to sit across the table, face-to-face, and share ideas. We need one another.

When you're intentional about reaching out to people, especially those outside your usual circle or tribe, you'll discover fresh insights. Independence may be the status quo, especially in the age of remote work, but don't settle. None of us can do this alone.

You might be one relationship or conversation away from a pivotal change in your life. Sometimes, we're so immersed in our projects that we fail to see the bigger picture. Never underestimate the value of proximity, of being around others who can provide wisdom and perspective. These interactions can be transformative.

Here are a few reasons collaboration is crucial for cultivating godly ambition.

Co-Laborers, Not Competitors

First, collaboration helps redirect our unhealthy competitive instincts into more productive and communal efforts. Coming from an athletic background, I've experienced firsthand the drive to dominate opponents, which doesn't always align with the principles of godly stewardship and service. By shifting from a mindset of scarcity (which views others as competitors) to one of abundance (which views others as potential collaborators), we not only temper our egos but also open ourselves to people's valuable perspectives.

I see my circle of Christian creators as allies for the same cause. And I seek every opportunity to learn from them, recognizing that together we can further the kingdom's message more effectively.

Another practical example is my ongoing passion for music. Despite other professional responsibilities, I can't let go of music creation. It's a part of me. Recently, I discussed with my friend Ray Rock a vision for a music collective that would support artists I've connected with. Instead of having me dive headfirst into writing camps and live albums, Ray suggested starting with a simpler, more manageable approach. He asked, "What is the micro version of it that you can start now?" This question was crucial because it encouraged me to consider smaller, more feasible steps that still align with my larger vision but require less immediate investment and risk.

Sometimes, collaborating catalyzes you to hit the gas and move faster. Other times, like my conversation with Ray Rock, it will slow you down, helping you avoid biting off more than you can chew. In either case, you need a sounding board—an objective third-party perspective to bring balance. Whenever possible, I strive to provide wise counsel to friends about their businesses, knowing firsthand the benefit I've received from others.

Collaboration in this context is not just about working together; it's about fostering meaningful relationships that challenge us to think differently and act more strategically. It moves us away from the need to dominate and toward a more communal, insightful approach that creates more lasting results.

Don't Let the Fire Die

Second, collaboration is immensely beneficial to godly ambition because it keeps the fire lit within us. We can often lose sight of our accomplishments or become too self-critical, letting impostor syndrome diminish our recognition of the work God is blessing. In such moments, having collaborators can be a lifeline—they may remind us of our capabilities and past successes and even help us recognize and address our blind spots. This dynamic is crucial when we feel bogged down by stress or when our endeavors aren't progressing as expected.

When everything shut down in 2020, I couldn't do live podcasts. Up to that point, not wanting to be a Christian YouTuber, I hadn't spoken too much about my faith. But with no one to interview, I decided to talk more about it. I'll never forget the day my friend KB, who's a pretty big Christian artist and podcaster, reached out.

He said, "Hey, you gotta keep doing this. We need your voice."

Coming from a friend and someone I looked up to, this meant the world to me. His encouragement affirmed a new direction I was unsure about. On my own, I might've given up, but thanks to his support (along with that of a few other friends), I was motivated to keep going.

In essence, collaboration acts as both a mirror reflecting our past achievements and a window showcasing our potential future successes. It reassures us, keeps us grounded, and pushes us to transcend our limits. The more we engage with others in our projects (and theirs), the more we can support one another's growth and continue to innovate meaningfully in our respective fields.

Collaboration fuels motivation, creates hope, and propels us forward.

OPENING DOORS

It all started with Felix, a professional skateboarder who reached out to me via Instagram. Following a service where he heard me preach at my church, our families went to lunch and hit it off. His wife is a designer for a major fashion brand, and together, they are well connected in the LA fashion scene—a rare feat for a devoted Christian and family man like Felix.

Through his introduction, I connected with Hali, a talented fashion designer, and we are now working together to bring a vision I had to life: a premium custom jacket made from Japanese salvaged denim, reversible with a nylon interior and a high-end heavy premium denim exterior. Hali's expertise has not only brought my idea into reality but also bolstered my confidence to innovate and take risks. His reassurance that my audience would appreciate this new venture, based on their reception of my past products, was crucial.

It's amazing how doors open through collaboration. On my own, I had no idea how to pursue this project, but by building friendships with others in different industries, I'm discovering new opportunities. Hali has not only expanded my creative horizons but also immersed me in a community of like-minded creatives committed to displaying God's beauty and goodness through our art.

Each step in this journey of collaboration has both fulfilled its immediate purpose and sown the seeds for future cooperative endeavors. When we collaborate, we are not just working on projects—we are potentially setting the stage for more relationships that could significantly impact our future. Just as my interactions with BrandMan Sean shifted the direction of my career, new relationships fostered through communal efforts can lead to transformative ideas and opportunities. This dynamic of expanding networks through collaboration not only enriches our professional lives but also aligns with our spiritual mission to advance God's kingdom.

Joint Ventures vs. Partnerships

A word of warning is in order here: It is crucial to distinguish fruitful collaborations from detrimental ones—the times you collaborate out of insecurity, or what I call "creative codependency." You're afraid to try something alone, so you team up with others. For the first fifteen years of my journey as an entrepreneur, I lived with this unhealthy dependency, constantly seeking partnerships not because they were helpful but because I was afraid to fail. I drifted from one rap group to another, from one label collective to the next, because I didn't believe I was capable of achieving success as a solo artist. This cycle not only stifled my personal growth but also held me back from financial independence.

Collaboration should be a choice made from a position of strength and clarity, not a necessity born from fear or inadequacy. While I continue to cherish collaborative projects and enjoy working with other artists, I am committed to ensuring that these connections are healthy and mutually beneficial. I encourage you, too, to approach collaboration with discernment. Engage with others because you genuinely value their contributions, not because you feel incapable of succeeding on your own. Ensure that each communal effort is a step toward mutual growth and success rather than a crutch that holds you back from realizing your full potential as a self-sufficient, confident creator.

Dave Ramsey critiques partnerships in his EntreLeadership resources[1] and notes that "the only ship that won't sail is a partnership,"[2] due to the common imbalances in contribution that often lead to resentment. Instead, he advocates for joint ventures, which are business arrangements "in which two or more parties agree to pool their resources for the purpose of accomplishing a specific task," while maintaining separate business interests.[3]

Joint ventures offer structured ways to collaborate without the pitfalls of traditional partnerships, setting clear roles and shared responsibilities. This approach minimizes the risks of creative codependency, allowing each participant to contribute equitably and maintain autonomy.

If you want to team up with someone, great! Many people start new businesses together—podcasts, merch lines, musical groups. Rather than forming a partnership, though, my advice is to launch a joint venture.

I love scouting new musical talents. In 2018, I discovered an artist named Paul Russell. We decided to make an album together, but instead of creating a new group, we maintained our individual identities. It was a collaboration, but not a business partnership. I was able to leverage my audience to introduce a new artist, and in exchange, I benefited from Paul's rapidly growing audience. He's since become one of the biggest artists on TikTok, and as of this writing, the music video for his single "Lil Boo Thang" has over thirty-six million views on YouTube.

ADVICE ON COLLABORATING

If you're wondering how to pursue meaningful collaborations, I'll give you my brief playbook. Whether you're just starting out or already have traction, these five principles will help you form the right business friendships in the right way.

1. BE A RELENTLESS INITIATOR

In the modern world, we're afraid of bothering others, so we leave our neighbors alone. We keep to ourselves. We don't want to be a burden. If you're a creator or entrepreneur, *this is wrong!* While it may feel countercultural or uncomfortable to initiate conversations—whether in person or through emails, phone calls, or DMs—it is up to *you* to seek out others. Don't expect collaborators to fall into your lap.

In today's isolated digital environment, social soft skills are often lacking. Don't succumb to this. Make your presence known. If you do, you'll be at a great advantage. Yes, it takes courage, but it's worth it. In the back of your mind, you might feel insecure, wondering if you come across as annoying or overbearing (more on that in a second). However, even if the worst happens and someone blows you off, so what? Now you know. On the flip side, your initiative might lead to a mutually beneficial connection.

Right now I'm planning my first summit, and to help make it successful, I reached out to a handful of pastor friends, asking them to bring some of their people. It feels vulnerable to ask, "Hey, can you do me a favor? I need you to bring a group to this conference so it's a success." To my surprise, though, almost every pastor I contacted, from churches of all sizes, said yes. Some even invited me to come speak at their churches to help promote the summit. Their warmth is a helpful reminder that it's worthwhile to initiate, even when it's uncomfortable.

Be willing to take the first step toward someone you respect and want to learn from. Initiate.

2. Whenever Possible, Ask for Warm Introductions

One of the best tactics to spark a new friendship is to ask someone you already know to introduce you to someone you *want* to know. Sure, you can send a cold DM or email. (Ironically, my editor at WaterBrook reached out this way, so sometimes it works!) But in most cases, you'll be ignored. It's not that people don't want to know you—it's that our world is oversaturated with information. It's hard to know whom to trust or who's reaching out only because they want something.

But having someone they know say "Hey, meet so-and-so; they're awesome" holds weight with people. It's a built-in vetting system that lets them know you're safe and trustworthy. So as often as you can, have friends introduce you to others. This not only opens the door, granting you access, but also sets the stage, building trust.

Don't hesitate to lean on the people you know. In return, be willing to provide warm introductions for others. In my opinion, there are few things as fun as connecting two people who I think will make great collaborators.

3. Strive to Bring Value

Sometimes the word *networking* brings to mind an obnoxious self-serving individual who endlessly begs for favors but rarely helps others. It's all about self. As soon as they get what they want, they're gone. It shouldn't need saying, but here it is anyway: *Don't be that person.*

Always start with how you can serve the other person, then overdeliver. Think of Jesus's mission statement: "Even the Son of Man did not come to be served, but to serve, and to give his life as a ransom for many" (Mark 10:45). If that's our Master's job description, shouldn't ours be the same? A great place to begin when meeting with someone new is simply to ask, "How can I serve or support you?" Don't be surprised if they lack an answer; many people are caught off guard by the question since so many relationships tend to be transactional. Give them a moment to process. Let them know that if anything comes to mind, you're willing and able to help.

If they *do* mention some way you can serve them, get after it. So long as it's within your boundaries (of time, finances, beliefs, and so forth), throw yourself into it wholeheartedly. Being valuable to someone is a good thing.

I've discovered that people find it most useful when we're willing to share our knowledge. And it feels good to be in a position to help people. As a practical example, I get messages all the time from aspiring creators who ask me to mentor them. Obviously, I can't coach twenty different people, so I tell them, "Hey, I can't hop on a call with you, but I'm here for any questions you have. Send me a voice memo, and I will respond as I can." This usually distills what they're truly looking to learn. If they want information, I'm an open book. Remember God's maxim: "It is more blessed to give than to receive" (Acts 20:35).

Be lavish in your helpfulness and conservative in your ask. Some people will milk it and move on. Be willing to take that risk. While the hope is mutual collaboration and benefit, even when the other person falls short, your service shows love for God and neighbor. Don't use someone for your own gain; seek to serve.

4. Look Outside Your Lane

When you're trying to collaborate, you'll intuitively look for others like you—people whose work, art, background, or field align with yours. Obviously, if you're an influencer on YouTube, you will connect with other YouTubers. If you're a barista, it's beneficial to hang out with and learn from other coffee experts. If you're a painter, you can glean a lot from fellow artists. If you're an athlete, it's wise to seek training from coaches who know your sport inside and out.

That said, there's much wisdom to be gained from collaborating with people who are very different from you. Those who have different skills and work in other industries than you do often possess the perspective you need to take your work to the next level. Think outside the box.

> What can an artist teach you about business?
> What can an influencer teach you about finance?
> How can a musician impact your writing?
> How might an elderly retiree speak into your entrepreneurial journey?
> How can someone from a different part of the world broaden your perspective?

Don't be so insular that you miss out on the treasure trove of wisdom outside your circle. In those diverse, unexpected friendships, you'll discover life-changing ideas.

5. Celebrate Their Wins

One of the most impactful ways to signal you care about someone—that you're not just in this friendship for yourself—is to applaud their work. The point is not flattery but intentionality. It's refreshing for them to have someone see and value what they've done without an ask or an underlying motive. So, cheer them on and express your gratitude for how their work or accomplishments have impacted you. This could involve sending an email or text, leaving a comment, mailing a handwritten note, or placing a phone call.

Remember, even those you look up to, who are further down the road professionally, struggle with self-doubt, discouragement, and setbacks. They expect to receive positivity when they help someone, so offer them the surprising gift of affirmation at other times, when they least expect it—when it's clear your only motivation is to bless them. As you sow encouragement into others, in time it will return to you. You won't regret it.

YOUR NEXT STEP

Take a moment and identify at least one person you've wanted to connect with but haven't. What's holding you back—fear, apathy, busyness? Without connection, there can't be collaboration. And without collaboration, your creative wings will be clipped. Relationship is fuel for godly ambition, so don't run on empty. When you link up with others, you're guaranteed to stand stronger, go further, and, honestly, have *way* more fun along the way.

9

Connect to Community

It's trendy nowadays to be a "self-made" person or a solopreneur—someone who ditches the entanglements of a team to run a one-person enterprise. Aspiring leaders spend thousands of dollars on personal growth, masterminds, coaching, and one-on-one mentorship, all in the name of improving themselves.

While I celebrate this interest in self-improvement, as a follower of Jesus, I can't help but notice a glaring gap in the modern approach to excellence: There is little talk about the church.

To the world, the church seems like a modest organization—filled with polite, well-meaning religious folks at best or judgmental, hypocritical charlatans at worst. In a sea of successful titans with multimillion-dollar portfolios, the church is set aside like a trinket from a bygone era. The real action, it's assumed, is elsewhere. The church should stay in its lane and focus on discipleship, not stick its nose in business or leadership.

This chapter is my pushback.

It's not hyperbolic to say that *every* aspect of my personal and professional growth has been dramatically catalyzed by the local church. Without it, my life would look completely different. And it's the same for you. As a Christian, your involvement in a local church will make or break your ability to fulfill your calling. Let me show you why.

WHY THE CHURCH?

Normally, we think about church as the place we worship, grow spiritually, and serve others. This is right, but there's more. The church has played a vital role in shaping my personal and spiritual journey. From my earliest days of serving on the sound team, setting up and tearing down equipment, to eventually teaching and leading various age groups, the church has provided me with opportunities to grow in humility, leadership, and relational skills. One of the most transformative aspects has been the accountability and support I've received through men's Bible studies and Financial Peace University (FPU), which taught me to manage my resources better and live in godly stewardship. These experiences deepened my faith, strengthened my character, and equipped me for the challenges of entrepreneurship and family life.

In the church, I've found a community offering practical wisdom and spiritual nourishment—not just for my personal life but for my professional life too. Since the gospel impacts every part of our lives, including how we think and act in the workplace, always be on the lookout for this type of vocational wisdom in your church community.

Here's how I've seen this play out.

A Place to Hone Your Gifts

Years ago, one of my best friends approached me, saying, "Hey, my church wants to start producing video announcements.

You have a camera, and you know how to edit in Final Cut Pro. Let's shoot a bunch of mock announcements. Maybe we can get you a job at the church."

For some reason, I agreed, but to be honest, I barely knew how to use my camera. For those who know about photography gear, it was a Canon T2i, so nothing fancy. We set everything up and shot some fake announcements, and when he showed the footage to the staff, they hired me. It turned out to be my best-paying job up to that point: $3,500 a month (an upgrade from my previous job, where I made $2,000 a month).

That job did more than pay the bills. It helped me recognize a valuable skill set I didn't know I had. God designed the church to be a safe place to discover and cultivate practical and spiritual gifts. Few of us know at a young age what we're good at—it's a learning process. Think about how many opportunities to explore your passions the church at large provides: audiovisual training, teaching and preaching, working with children, set building, singing, playing in a band, event planning, evangelizing, providing hospitality, and engaging in service projects, missions, widow care, ministry to those with disabilities, foster care and adoption, fundraising, administration, community and renovation projects, project management, and so much more. Unlike any other organization or movement, the church offers an unmatched menu of options in a safe, nurturing space—all of which improve your spiritual, relational, and vocational health.

Every gift I've developed was incubated in my local church. While on staff, one of the most pivotal skills I learned was video broadcasting. We'd just started live streaming services, and I was tasked with setting up and managing our weekly broadcasts. I had to learn about video switchers, camera angles, and live audio mixing—skills I had never explored. The church provided me with a safe space to experiment, learn from mistakes, and refine my technical skills without the high-pressure stakes of a professional studio. I had no clue my growing knowledge of video production would later become vital in my transition to YouTube, where I now run a multicamera setup to produce content for hundreds of thousands of viewers.

Teaching at church also played a huge role in honing my communication abilities. I taught many age groups—from children to teenagers to young adults—which challenged me to adapt my content and delivery based on the listeners. This versatility has served me well as a content creator who aims to reach a diverse audience.

The church environment was ideal for this kind of skill development because it encouraged growth without the fear of failure. It was a place where I could experiment, receive feedback, and improve both spiritually and professionally. The church fosters a culture of grace and support, making it a safe space to try new things. Where else can you practice on expensive equipment, be allowed to fail, and learn skills in the process? Through serving in the church, I developed soft skills like communication, teamwork, problem-solving, and leadership—abilities that are invaluable not just in ministry but in every area of life.

Whether it's learning a technical skill like video broadcasting or honing your expertise through teaching, the church offers the chance to grow in a low-pressure environment where mistakes are seen as part of the learning process. The focus is on service and personal development, allowing you to explore and develop talents that may otherwise remain untapped.

Part of our mission is to call out gifts in one another. Hebrews 10:24 tells us as the church to "spur one another on toward love and good deeds." We need the clarity and boldness of others who can say, "I see this gift in you." Many times, other people will see a gift or ability in you before you see it in yourself.

Mentorship

Motivational speaker Jim Rohn is widely attributed with saying, "We are the average of the five people we spend the most time with." One of the greatest gifts I've received from the church is mentorship. When I struggled financially, people I met through small groups or serving opportunities, including entrepreneurs and middle-class or upper-middle-class folks, shared business tips and budgeting advice with me. Now, as an entrepreneur, I support those who are less fortunate and mentor younger individuals aspiring to improve their lives. When I was single, attending church gave me insights from newly engaged couples, enabling me to learn from their experiences and mistakes. As I transitioned through engagement, marriage, and parenting, I was always a step behind someone I could learn from.

This life-on-life mentorship is typically something you have to pay for. Access to masterminds, cohorts, or one-on-one coaching isn't cheap. But in the church, you can chop it up with people from all industries, walks, and stages of life *for free*. This unfettered access to wisdom is unparalleled outside God's family. Perhaps the mentors you've been looking for are already sitting beside you every Sunday—you just haven't recognized it yet.

When I was at a juncture in my career, trying to decide between music and YouTube, I asked my pastor Jeff for advice. "There are two directions I can go," I said. "I can keep developing artists through my music label, or I can develop my channel. What do you think?"

I'll never forget his response: "Well, what would be best for your family?"

That simple question was a game changer. As much as I loved the music industry, it had taken a toll on my health and family. YouTube would allow me to be home most days—to be a more present father and husband. Without Jeff's counsel, I'm not sure I would have seen the path forward so clearly.

We tend to overthink mentorship. The best advice doesn't always come with a high price tag from someone with an impressive title; sometimes it's a one-off comment, a well-timed question, or a kind word that reminds you of God's presence. It's two moms commiserating about sleepless nights with babies, trading best practices in the parking lot. It's a CEO taking an interest in a young professional, inviting them to the office to observe for a day. It's a pastor sitting with an engaged couple, talking them through healthy strategies for conflict resolution. It's the person sitting next to you who discovers a shared passion and offers you a warm introduction to someone you've been wanting to connect with.

Wisdom leaks out in the ebbs and flows of community, in side conversations, over coffee, in small groups. While there's value in formal coaching relationships, one hour per month on a Zoom call with a guru can't deliver nearly as much as a weekly rhythm of in-person connection in a diverse community. Don't buy the narrative that church is for prudes and potlucks. For those with eyes to see, it's a master class full of mentors.

Dr. David McClelland discovered that the people we associate with determine as much as 95 percent of our success or failure in life.[1] As Scripture teaches, "Walk with the wise and become wise, for a companion of fools suffers harm" (Proverbs 13:20). So much of what we learn is caught rather than taught. Whom you hang out with is who you become.

If you're surrounded by friends who engage deeply with the Bible, pray regularly, and serve others, you're more likely to adopt these behaviors yourself. Contemporary psychology underscores what Scripture has *always* taught about human behavior.

A psychological phenomenon called "the Pygmalion effect" explains that people who have higher expectations placed on them tend to perform better. The most famous study of the Pygmalion effect was conducted by Robert Rosenthal and Lenore Jacobson at an elementary school in 1965.[2] Teachers were told that certain students scored higher on an intelligence test, though in reality they were no different from their peers. At the end of the school year, these students' IQ scores were much higher than their classmates'. Why? Because, unconsciously, the teachers held them to higher standards, gave them more attention, and encouraged them to perform at a peak level.

Similarly, the church is a place where life-on-life encouragement, accountability, and investment occur. In community, we're held to higher standards. All of this contributes to our growth and performance.

Consider how Paul tells his mentee Timothy to "fan into flame the gift of God, which is in you through the laying on of my hands. For the Spirit God gave us does not make us timid, but gives us power, love and self-discipline" (2 Timothy 1:6–7). You can hear Paul setting the bar high for Timothy ("Don't be timid"), while at the same time encouraging him ("You're gifted and filled with the Spirit").

My church family believes the best about who I am and who God is still shaping me into. If not for my local church, I wouldn't have met mentors who taught me how to build a business. Nor would I have met the couples who were a few seasons ahead of my wife and me and provided guidance, especially in our first few years of marriage. Nor would I spend so much time around people vastly different from me—who teach me about the diverse beauty of the kingdom.

Randy Craig is one of the mentors who played a pivotal role in my faith journey. When my wife and I were newlyweds, we joined a home group that met every Tuesday night at Randy's place. His home was always warm and inviting, with a fire crackling in the fireplace and a sense of peace in the air. The Bible study itself lasted about an hour, but most nights we stayed long after, often until midnight, talking about life over cookies and tea. Randy and his wife never preached at us—they simply lived alongside us, leading by example and letting us into their lives. For two young people coming from single-parent homes, it was a huge blessing to experience their home, witness their marriage, and receive their wisdom.

Randy has always been a source of encouragement, showing up to every one of my rap shows with his family, even though rap music wasn't really his thing. He's a brilliant piano player and a humble author who has written evangelistic discipleship resources that have reached millions, though he's never put his name on them.

Recently, when I ran into trouble with manufacturing my prayer journals, Randy stepped in to help. He had spent two decades cultivating relationships with overseas manufacturers, and he quickly connected me with one that was more efficient and much cheaper than the one I was using. His generosity cut out the middleman I had been relying on, saving me time, money, and effort. What could have taken me hundreds of hours to figure out he shared with me in one simple conversation.

The overflow of doing life together, like we did with Randy and his wife, can have profound impacts on our lives. It's in late-night conversations, shared experiences, and consistent encouragement that deeper connections form and life-changing support emerges. The truth is, every successful person stands on the shoulders of giants—mentors, friends, and leaders—who helped elevate them to achieve more than they ever could on their own. Randy's influence in my life, from his quiet faithfulness to his willingness to share his wisdom and resources, is a perfect example of how those relationships can ripple into every area of our lives.

I want to be clear: Our primary motivation in building relationships in the local church isn't to get something *from* others but to do life *alongside* them. However, as you invest in others, you'll be surprised at the tangible blessings that come from these friendships.

In the digital age, we tend to exist in like-minded echo chambers. There's value to spending time with peers, but a life filled with people just like us is unfulfilling. Beautifully, the church places us into a diverse ecosystem—filled with people from different backgrounds, ethnicities, income levels, and life stages. This is uncomfortable in the best way, softening our hearts and increasing our awareness of God's multifaceted world.

Going to church is about more than the pragmatic benefits outlined in this chapter. It's about what you can give, not just what you receive. If you're serious about channeling your ambition for God's glory and the good of others, let's talk about serving.

SERVING

While it's common to talk about discovering gifts and mentorship in the church, an overlooked gift of the church that is foundational for godly ambition is *serving others*. For most of us, service falls into the "spiritual" bucket, but we don't connect it to our professional goals. However, you can spend a lifetime increasing your competence, but if you neglect your character in the process, what's the point? If there's one thing that sets godly ambition apart from selfish ambition, it's a willingness to serve.

As an entrepreneur, I've found serving to be one of the most transformative aspects of my life. It's a two-way street, allowing me to develop useful skills *and* benefit others. If I hadn't been plugged into a local church that gave me opportunities to serve, I wouldn't be where I am. I've been involved in almost every capacity at the church. A highlight was last summer, when I had the privilege of serving in Sunday school with the one-year-old babies. It was a profound experience.

As I've mentioned before, when I first started attending church, I served on the sound setup and teardown crew. Eventually, I joined the sound team. I've taught almost every grade, from junior high to high school to young adults. I've stacked chairs, cleaned bathrooms, and vacuumed classrooms. Serving like this has not only kept me grounded but also provided opportunities to build relationships. Some of my dearest friends and mentors came into my life while we served together.

American Christianity leans toward consumption: *What can this church offer me?* Although there's nothing wrong with evaluating how a church might meet your needs, an equally important question is, *What can I offer this church?* When we choose to serve, it curbs our tendency to consume, mobilizing us to get busy for the benefit of the community.

So, what does serving have to do with godly ambition?

Apart from Jesus, ambition is prone to produce pride. In a world that idolizes status—whether you're an influencer, entrepreneur, celebrity, or leader—entitlement subtly creeps in. If small tasks start to feel beneath us, service shakes us back to reality. It points us to Jesus, who humbly served those around him. It aligns our ambition with God's heart.

It's incredible to consider that Jesus, the eternal Son of God, "did not come to be served, but to serve" (Mark 10:45). He knelt with a towel around his waist to wash his disciples' feet (John 13:1–17). He gave up his life for his friends and enemies alike. If *he* served, how can we do anything less?

The powers of this world are too strong to fight with willpower alone. It's only in the trenches of service, with dirt on our hands and compassion in our hearts, that the strangleholds of fame, success, and selfishness release their grip. Something happens in your soul on Sunday morning when, despite the long week you've had, you drag yourself out of bed and show up to church early to set up chairs. There's a joy that comes when you give up a Saturday to serve the needy in your community alongside your brothers and sisters. And there's a palpable holiness in a room of toddlers who are squirming and half listening to the Bible story you're telling from the front of the classroom.

Faithfulness in Little Things

In so many visions of career growth and self-improvement, service is entirely lacking. It's respected in an obligatory way, as something to do in your free time, but it's not viewed as integral to success. Yet in Jesus's kingdom, it's a top priority. It's the path to greatness.

As Proverbs says, "humility comes before honor" (15:33; 18:12). It's easy to work hard in pursuit of recognition, honor, and platform. It's much harder to be faithful in the little things. But this is exactly what God requires, as Luke 16 teaches us: "Whoever can be trusted with very little can also be trusted with much, and whoever is dishonest with very little will also be dishonest with much. So if you have not been trustworthy in handling worldly wealth, who will trust you with true riches? And if you have not been trustworthy with someone else's property, who will give you property of your own?" (verses 10–12).

The practice of service fundamentally shifts our focus from pursuing success and wealth for their own sakes to submitting these desires to God's timing and will. This involves stewarding well what we have been entrusted with, regardless of the season we are in. As Jesus explains in Luke 16, being faithful in the small things is a precondition for being entrusted with greater things. Before we aspire to more, we must develop the character and discipline necessary to handle the responsibilities in our hands. Often, we desire more before we're ready to manage even the little we have, overlooking the importance of faithful stewardship.

We often hear the adage "God only gives you what you can handle" in reference to hardship and persecution. While this idea isn't necessarily true in that context, it does apply to success and calling: Because he loves you, God won't give you a gift if he knows it will spoil you.

Our calling is to embody the servant leadership modeled by Jesus Christ. He washed the feet of his disciples, an act that epitomized humility and service. In the same way, we are to use our talents and gifts not to elevate ourselves but to serve those around us. By doing so, we not only fulfill our divine mandate but also contribute to a more just, compassionate, and thriving world.

The Benefits of Service

Just as we saw with mentorship, modern psychology has begun to confirm what ancient scriptural truths have long taught us: Serving others is good for you, not just in a spiritual sense, but holistically. Numerous studies show that volunteering boosts mental health, increases life satisfaction, and reduces rates of depression and anxiety.[3] When you're focused on serving others, you have less time to dwell on your own problems.

Additionally, serving others can significantly reduce stress and feelings of loneliness. Engaging in volunteer activities is associated with a "helper's high," a phenomenon where serving releases endorphins—the brain's natural pain relievers—creating a sense of well-being and lowering stress levels.[4] This benefit is especially important in today's fast-paced, isolated world. Even though I work with a team of three, all crammed into my studio, digital work can be lonely. Our habit is to take a walk in the middle of the day, which provides some fresh air and time to connect beyond work responsibilities.

Whether or not you work a remote job, you live in an individualized age that naturally pulls you away from community toward independence. If you're more of an introvert, you might think, *Great! That's exactly what I want.* Even so, God has created you to thrive alongside others, which is a major upside of serving regularly.

Moreover, volunteering forges friendships. Especially in larger churches, it's easy to feel lost in the masses, unseen and unknown. You can show up each Sunday without running into the same person twice. This is a tragedy—church is a place to be known, not somewhere to blend in anonymously. Serving on a team immediately connects you to a circle of people. As a group, you can invest in one another's lives, strategize about your ministry goals, and problem solve (all skills you can apply elsewhere). For young people, volunteering introduces them to mentors, provides an environment to develop social skills, and solidifies their sense of belonging. For older adults, volunteering offers a valuable avenue to stay connected and share their wisdom.

All these benefits of serving are wonderful, but I think the deeper motivation should stem from Jesus's teachings. After washing his disciples' feet, he said, "A new command I give you: Love one another. As I have loved you, so you must love one another" (John 13:34). Jesus served us and sacrificed his life for us, and he explains that this is the way we must love one another. Serving isn't only about meeting needs in the church; it's the way of God's kingdom. It's how we align our hearts with his. Jesus continued, "By this everyone will know that you are my disciples, if you love one another" (verse 35). Our service is an expression of our love. And you can love people only when you do life *with* them.

Living in California, I *love* redwood trees. They're "the tallest trees on earth, reaching more than 350 feet high." Standing among them, looking upward, makes me feel like I'm dwelling on another planet. You'd expect these giants to have deep roots, but surprisingly, "a typical redwood's root system is only 6 to 12 feet deep." So how do they stand so strong, withstanding "powerful winds and floods"? Here's their secret: They extend their roots outward, "up to 100 feet wide from the trunk," each tree intertwining its roots with all the others in the grove.[5]

This is how God has designed *you* to thrive—not alone, trying to establish your own foundation, but *connected,* locking arms with others. It's only when your life is embedded in a church community that you can give love like Christ's as well as receive it. If the tallest trees in the world can't stand alone, neither can you.

DON'T GIVE UP

Today, a lot of "connection" happens digitally—via Zoom screens, online courses, and pricey masterminds. Yet despite our technologically connected existence, loneliness has reached dismal proportions.[6] Turns out, there's no substitute for living life together, face-to-face, in person. We are better together—not in the glow of devices but in the embodied warmth of real life.

Much has been written about the impact of technology on mental health, as well as the importance of in-person connection, so I won't belabor those points here. Instead, I want to highlight the impact of community on your calling.

Hebrews 10:25 tells us to keep meeting together as the church. It's always tempting to drift into isolation, but we'll never fulfill our calling apart from the family of God. Without the nurture and care of a parent, no child can thrive. And without the support of your brothers and sisters in the faith, you won't make it. So, even though it's challenging some days, Hebrews encourages us to keep at it. Don't give up on church.

There are a lot of reasons people stop going to church—more than I have time to cover here. It could be a lack of desire or motivation, an unusually busy season at work, or the demands of a child's club or team. Whatever the case, I encourage you to think deeply about the implications of pushing church attendance to the back burner.

"Be alert and of sober mind. Your enemy the devil prowls around like a roaring lion looking for someone to devour" (1 Peter 5:8). This is a striking image: Our enemy actively searches for ways to destroy us. Think about a lion's hunting strategy. It stalks the herd, looking for the youngest or weakest animal to single out, then tries to isolate it from the rest of the group. The lesson is this: When you're alone, you're the most vulnerable. If Satan can convince you that church is optional, that you're too busy to make it a priority, you'll basically be separated from the herd. It's a dangerous place to be.

Please hear me: This is not a guilt trip. As someone who toured for years as an artist and who currently travels a lot for work, my church attendance is not always exemplary. You're in good company. However, whenever I'm able (which is most weeks), church is a non-negotiable for me and my family. Attending is an act of obedience; it's a way to live out Jesus's call to "love one another." There's always a cost when you commit to community, but in return, we have received more than I can recount here. This reflects God's heart; when we trust him enough to invest our lives in *his* will, he blesses it. It will be the same for you.

WHAT ABOUT CHURCH HURT?

As we wrap up this chapter, we need to address the elephant in the room: church hurt. Some of you are hesitant to plug in to a church because you've been betrayed, judged, or ignored. Perhaps a leader you trusted let you down. Maybe you're jaded from the endless headlines about the latest church scandals—it feels like pastors are falling like dominoes.

When I first gave my life to Jesus, I helped launch a Bible study and open mic night at my church. Sometimes as many as one hundred kids would show up. I'd bring all the leftover pizza from my job at Pizza Hut. It was awesome. A lot of kids who came didn't go to church, so it wasn't uncommon for them to smoke weed in the parking lot. I'd asked the executive pastor for permission to host these events, and he'd said yes. However, once the senior pastor found out about it, he immediately shut it down. When I asked to meet with him, he refused to have a conversation with me. He wouldn't even let us host a final meeting. It was just over. I want to be charitable, but no matter how you slice it, this pastor's actions were questionable. I mean, who turns away one hundred unchurched kids? What an opportunity to share the gospel! Instead, he chose suspicion over compassion. That might seem like a minor incident, but as a new Christian, it affected me.

If a painful church experience has wounded you—if you feel angry, let down, or hurt—I want to remind you of the heart of Jesus. Have you ever noticed who Jesus was the hardest on? It wasn't the prostitutes, tax collectors, or thieves. You might assume he would rail against the riffraff, telling them to shape up. While Jesus does clean people up, he first welcomes them *as they are*. He shepherds them, showing them a better way. It may surprise you, but Jesus's harshest words were aimed at spiritual leaders—the pastors, theologians, and clergy of his day—who abused their power in God's name. Listen to his rebuke of these corrupt leaders:

> Woe to you, teachers of the law and Pharisees, you hypocrites! You shut the door of the kingdom of heaven in people's faces. You yourselves do not enter, nor will you let those enter who are trying to.
>
> Woe to you, teachers of the law and Pharisees, you hypocrites! You travel over land and sea to win a single convert, and when you have succeeded, you make them twice as much a child of hell as you are. . . .
>
> Woe to you, teachers of the law and Pharisees, you hypocrites! You clean the outside of the cup and dish, but inside they are full of greed and self-indulgence. Blind Pharisee! First clean the inside of the cup and dish, and then the outside also will be clean. (Matthew 23:13–15, 25–26)

If you've been betrayed by a leader or person in the church, God sees it. He mourns with you, weeps with you, and fights for you. The problem of bad leaders among God's people stretches back to the Old Testament, where God told Ezekiel to "prophesy against the shepherds of Israel; prophesy and say to them: 'This is what the Sovereign LORD says: Woe to you shepherds of Israel who only take care of yourselves! Should not shepherds take care of the flock?'" (34:2).

Then God speaks these comforting words:

> I myself will search for my sheep and look after them. As a shepherd looks after his scattered flock when he is with them, so will I look after my sheep. I will rescue them from all the places where they were scattered on a day of clouds and darkness. I will bring them out from the nations and gather them from the countries, and I will bring them into their own land. I will pasture them on the mountains of Israel, in the ravines and in all the settlements in the land. I will tend them in a good pasture, and the mountain heights of Israel will be their grazing land. There they will lie down in good grazing land, and there they will feed in a rich pasture on the mountains of Israel. I myself will tend my sheep and have them lie down, declares the Sovereign LORD. I will search for the lost and bring back the strays. I will bind up the injured and strengthen the weak, but the sleek and the strong I will destroy. I will shepherd the flock with justice. (verses 11–16)

This is God's heart for anyone wrestling with church hurt: *He wants to be your shepherd.* He's seeking you out, determined to bring you back into the fold. To protect you from predators. To heal your wounds and nurse you back to health. To enact justice on your behalf. I can't explain why he's allowed you to walk through such pain. But as someone who grew up with an alcoholic mom and absentee dad and who survived sexual abuse from a group of older boys in my neighborhood, I'm here to tell you: *Healing is a slow process, but it's possible.* It might feel like ditching church is the safe option, but to live apart from God's family will only prolong your pain and deepen your loneliness.

I don't want to diminish the depths of your hurt. However, I still believe we're called as God's children to be part of his family. It might frighten or even repulse you to think about integrating into a church again. That's okay; take your time.

There is no perfect church. So, I want to challenge you: What would it look like for you to actively engage in a local church again? What's holding you back? If you're in a healthy place at a thriving church, how can you come alongside those who are doubting and hurting?

A PLACE TO BELONG

Community will always be messy (because people are involved), but let's end on a note of hope. Not some cheap, "look the other way and pretend everything's fine" optimism, but a serious look at some of God's promises about participating in his family. Like any family, the church has issues. But make no mistake: God loves you, and since he's given you the church, you can trust it's a good gift.

For a moment, allow God's promises to wash over you. Wherever you are in your journey, this is the Lord's heart for you:

> **Psalm 133:1:** "How good and pleasant it is when God's people live together in unity!" Be reminded today: God has blessings for those who commit to his family. You need strong believers around you to live out your calling. You need encouragers and

challengers, models in the faith and younger Christians to mentor.

Proverbs 27:17: "As iron sharpens iron, so one person sharpens another." Be reminded today: God wants to use fellow Christians to hone your gifts, sharpen your skills, and expand your dreams. Receive their wisdom; seek it out.

Hebrews 13:7: "Remember your leaders, who spoke the word of God to you. Consider the outcome of their way of life and imitate their faith." Be reminded today that not all shepherds are self-serving or abusive. Though the headlines spotlight corruption, countless churches are led by humble, faithful, loving shepherds who want to help you follow Jesus. They're ready to walk alongside you, teach you, and care for you. Though Christ is our ultimate leader, he's put others in your circle who can model what it looks like to follow him.

My friend, if you want to do great things for the kingdom of God, build something that lasts, and grow spiritually and professionally, invest in a local church. Show up as an eager giver and grateful receiver. God has given you a family to help you live out your purpose. Find your place in it, and find great joy in the journey.

10

Pray Boldly

"Pray as though everything depended on God, and work as though everything depended on you."[1] This quote encapsulates everything in this book, but it's especially relevant to this chapter, which tackles the importance of prayer.

You might wonder, *Is prayer relevant to a book on ambition?* In a culture that glorifies the hustle, talking to God holds little weight. As followers of Jesus, though we know better, it's still tempting to try to achieve through our own efforts alone. The key word there is *alone*. As Christians, we *are* called to work with all our strength—to give it our best. Prayer is not an excuse to sit back and hope it works out. On the flip side, our sincere efforts must flow from a life of dependence, where we acknowledge the outcome is in *his* hands. It's in this tension between trusting and working that godly ambition thrives.

PRAYER IN OUR STORY

Ever since my wife and I got married in 2008, I've had a dream to be self-employed, creating enough financial stability to allow her to stay home and homeschool our children. We prayed about this goal even before we were married, but to be honest, the first few years were anything but easy.

Initially, I secured a job at the YMCA, running their recording studio at an after-school program. I saw this as a bridge to pursuing music full-time. Back then, being an independent Christian rapper wasn't considered a viable career, so I figured it was best to start somewhere. Right around that time, the 2008 recession struck, slashing donations to the YMCA and, consequently, our budget. My hours were drastically cut, reducing my nearly full-time hours to a scant fifteen hours a week. Instead of fostering musical talent in the teen center, I was demoted to running the snack shop. It was demoralizing.

The timing couldn't have been worse. Just as I was about to get married, my financial stability crumbled. The income I had counted on to secure an apartment for us evaporated, and finding work became increasingly difficult. Yet amid this upheaval, prayer remained our anchor. I shared our struggles with a close-knit community of fellow Christian rappers online, seeking their prayers and support. Despite living with my mother (no newlyweds' dream) and juggling multiple jobs, we persisted in prayer. We meticulously recorded each prayer—a practice that not only strengthened our faith but also left a tangible record of our pleas and hopes.

We ended up living with my mom for our first year of marriage, though we initially expected it to be just a few months. It was humbling to try to find our footing as a new couple under my mother's roof. When we *finally* moved into our own apartment, we decided to tackle our financial debt head-on. At the start, we believed we were about $45,000 in the hole, spread across car notes, student loans, and credit cards. So, you can imagine our horror when we discovered I was legally liable for an additional $65,000 from a condo I had co-signed with my mom that had gone into foreclosure amid the housing bubble crash.

This discovery knocked the wind out of me. Faced with a total debt of $110,000, bankruptcy seemed the only conceivable option. However, instead of giving in to despair, we turned again to prayer and the practical steps of Dave Ramsey's Financial Peace principles. We diligently worked through the baby steps, and within eighteen months, we were debt-free.

I started a new job working with adults with developmental disabilities, and my wife reduced her workload to one full-time job. One step at a time, we inched toward our goal. Our dream for me to become a self-employed creative, supporting her as a stay-at-home mom, seemed distant but attainable. So, we continued to pray.

As we emerged debt-free, the financial burden eased, and my focus shifted back to my first passion—music. I prayed with an open heart, "Lord, you know my heart. I'd really love to do music full-time. I don't know how it's possible with a young family, but if that's not your will, I'm totally cool with it." Despite the uncertainty, an opportunity arose to work as the media guy at my church. Concurrently, I launched Kings Dream Entertainment, began producing other artists, and started touring more. Soon, my income from music rivaled that of my day job.

When our first son was born, my church role provided stability and taught me a lot about live streaming, public speaking, and content creation. Thankfully, it allowed my wife to fulfill her aspiration to be a stay-at-home mom. However, as my music career accelerated, it began to clash increasingly with my responsibilities at the church. Traveling for shows nearly every month, I felt tension mounting between my dual commitments. The strain reached a peak when I was returning from the SXSW music festival. At a diner in New Mexico, I called my wife—a new mother, at home with our six-month-old son—and asked, "Can we pray about me putting in my two-week notice?"

Her response surprised me. "There's nothing to pray about. Come home and put in your two-week notice." After years of continual prayer, it was time to put it all on the line. We felt God's blessing to transition to full-time entrepreneurship. On one hand, it was intimidating, but after months of discerning God's will, we entered that transition with peace and confidence.

We were ready for this transition, fortified by God's faithfulness and our diligent savings, which included six months of living expenses. If all else failed, I could drive for Uber. As much as this was a leap of faith, we had also meticulously prepared to support this major life change. It was more than a financial decision; it was a step of faith into the future we believed God had prepared for us.

In this season, how might prayer reshape your perspective? Have you been pouring out your requests to God or striving in your own strength? Do you believe, deep in your bones, that prayer impacts your calling? Have you connected your waiting (in prayer) to your doing?

THREE LIES HINDERING YOUR PRAYER LIFE

As someone who *loves* to charge ahead and set the bar high, I'll be honest: Prayer is a habit that doesn't come naturally to me. I've had to learn it over time (and I'm *still* learning). As we'll explore in a moment, the world we live in is antithetical to a life of prayer. We're so busy and distracted that it feels inconvenient. An impractical luxury. Not only that, but Satan loves to convince you prayer isn't effective or feasible. There are three lies circulating today to derail your prayer life. Let's face them head-on:

Lie 1: You Can Succeed Alone

Hustle culture appeals to our desire for independence. The reigning message is, "You got this! You can accomplish anything. Seize your dreams." Optimistic self-help strokes your ego but burdens your soul. The oldest lie in history is that you can achieve contentment apart from God. It's how the ancient serpent deceived Adam and Eve, and it's the same deception he uses today. He'll point your gaze at something you want, then convince you to abuse yourself to get it. Prayer gets pushed to the back burner; it stops being a priority, and before long, it feels totally powerless.

Don't buy it. You were created by God to depend on him. "Unless the LORD builds the house, the builders labor in vain" (Psalm 127:1). Likewise, Jesus says, "Apart from me you can do nothing" (John 15:5). All success comes from God's hand. Rather than pioneering your own path in your own power, accept God's invitation to partner with him.

Lie 2: Your Practical Life Is Separate from Your Spiritual Life

In modern life, we tend to put spiritual things in one category: church, prayer, small groups, Bible reading, etc. Then we make a separate grouping for the "practical" things, which include everyday tasks like career planning, laundry, commuting, and meal prepping.

Based on these categories, we think that to *really* accomplish something, we need to roll up our sleeves, not get on our knees. Ambition is about what we *do*, not what we pray. Though we might esteem prayer with our lips, if we're honest, it's an afterthought akin to a good luck charm: Maybe it makes a difference, but then again, maybe it doesn't.

This is why it's so important to be saturated in Scripture—to remind ourselves that God is active in everyday affairs. If God cared only about spiritual things, why did he take on flesh and become a human? If physical things are unspiritual, why has God promised to free creation "from its bondage to decay" (Romans 8:21)? God's own commitment to redeeming the tangible world disproves the myth that spiritual things are greater than physical things. He cares about *all* of creation, and so should we.

It seems the world and our everyday lives are far more spiritual than we think.

LIE 3: YOU NEED RESULTS *NOW*, NOT LATER

A challenging aspect of prayer is that it often involves waiting. The process of prayer takes time, and in an age of instant gratification, this can feel maddening. We're trained to order coffee, then pick it up five minutes later. If we want some gadget in the next few hours, we can pay a little extra and someone will deliver it to our doorstep. Thus, our avoidance of prayer is often an attempted shortcut—a refusal to wait for God to deliver an answer in his timing. In the digital age, God's response feels slow.

It's difficult to be patient when the rent is due and business is dwindling. When we're desperate for direction but the journey feels aimless. When we long to hear from God, but he's silent. Rather than waiting on a divine solution, we take matters into our own hands.

In the modern world, waiting feels like wasted time. But not so fast (pun intended) . . . In God's kingdom, waiting is where character is forged and wisdom is gained. I love this quote: "Give me six hours to chop down a tree and I will spend the first four sharpening the axe."[2] Prayer sharpens our spiritual and mental axes, preparing us to receive God's answer. At times, his greatest kindness is telling us to sit tight. In the moment, we can't see it, especially when we're driven to achieve, but in the waiting, he's sharpening us. Better to be God's battle-ax than a dull blade.

PRAYER *IS* PRACTICAL

A lot of Christians struggle with prayer. For some, the challenge is consistency. Others are unsure what to pray. Some feel let down that God hasn't spoken in the way they hoped or answered a desperate prayer. Maybe you're a pragmatist—really good at organizing, leading, and administrating—but it's difficult to slow down and sit in God's presence.

Wherever you find yourself in life—whether you're launching a business, working for a company, or raising kids—you'll be tempted to listen to other voices more than God's voice. I say this to help you, not to shame you. Life's pressures are heavy, and at times it will feel like prayer isn't easing the burden at all.

In such moments, rather than dropping to our knees, we just run harder. Even if God is prompting you to pick up the pace or take a second job, don't neglect the power of prayer. It's a spiritual act, yes, but it's also *practical*. God, who created the heavens and the earth and has numbered the hairs on your head, is the one who will provide.

My first five years as a full-time entrepreneur were financially challenging. But through it all, we never lacked food, always managed to pay our rent and bills on time, and figured out how to handle our taxes, even though saving was tough and we significantly depleted our six-month reserve. As our financial situation began to tighten to a point of real concern, my music income started to grow, along with my YouTube channel. This timely increase allowed me to build a team to help me scale my operations. Now more than a decade since I made the pivotal decision to quit my day job, I can look back and see the enormous role that prayer has played throughout this entire journey. It wasn't just about praying in those fork-in-the-road moments, asking God whether to go left or right; it was about maintaining a consistent dialogue with God while trusting in his timing. Praying continually frees you from anxiety so you can actively do your part, knowing God will do his.

Prayer didn't just change our circumstances; it changed *us*. I'm seeing God answer prayers today that I started praying more than twenty years ago when my wife and I first began dating. By God's grace, prayer has steadily reshaped my desires: I don't care nearly as much about being famous or successful as I did when I was younger. Every time I see God come through, it emboldens me to *keep praying*. It creates a holy momentum.

I want to introduce you to a simple habit that's transformed my prayer life: prayer journaling.

Prayer Journaling

In the quiet of the morning, while the world is still waking up, I take time to commune with God through my prayer journal. As I've mentioned before, this practice has become a foundational aspect of my spiritual routine. It is a time of reflection, request, and remembrance that aligns my day with God's presence and purposes.

Writing down my prayers in a journal serves multiple purposes. First and foremost, it helps me maintain consistency. A physical journal also acts as a tangible reminder to pause and engage with God amid the busyness of life. More importantly, it allows me to document my conversations with God. This is more than recordkeeping—it slows my thoughts and helps me articulate my requests and praises more clearly. It makes my prayer time an active dialogue where I'm not just speaking into the silence but laying down words that bear witness to my spiritual journey.

The act of writing down prayers ties deeply into the biblical theme of remembrance. Scripture repeatedly calls for the people of God to remember his deeds, his promises, and his laws. The psalmist finds himself in a spiritually dry place, thirsting for God "as the deer pants for streams of water" (Psalm 42:1). In his turmoil, he recalls the times he led the procession to the house of God with joy and praise (verse 4). This act of remembrance is not passive; it actively fosters renewal and reconnection with God.

The issue with the present is it feels so permanent. When faced with trials or dry spells, it's easy to feel as if they will never end. However, by maintaining records of our prayers and God's responses over time, we can look back and see the patterns of

God's faithfulness. Remembering how God moved in the past offers not just comfort but a robust hope that he will move again in the future. This remembrance is transformative, shifting our perspective from what currently is to what can be, underpinned by the certainty of God's unchanging character.

Every day, I walk through four basic steps in my prayer journal, modeled after the Lord's Prayer. If you're interested in learning more, I've created a prayer journal that has helped thousands of people connect with God. You can check it out at blessgod.shop.

Four Simple Steps

Again, my daily prayer time is deeply influenced by the prototype Jesus provided in the Lord's Prayer, found in Matthew 6:9–13. There's no better model than the one Jesus taught his disciples when they asked him how to pray. The basic flow is adoration, intercession, supplication, and reflection. In a journal or on a piece of paper, write down those four words, leaving space in between to write down your thoughts.

Take as much or as little time to journal as you'd like. When people ask me for advice about how long to pray, I try not to be prescriptive. The truth is, *all of us* can spend more time praying, but give yourself grace. If it's five minutes every morning, God is honored by that. If it's fifteen, twenty, thirty minutes—wonderful. The vital thing is to pray.

Let's walk through each part.

1. Adoration: Give Thanks to God

Each session begins by writing out praise reports and acknowledging the things I am grateful for. The Lord's Prayer begins with a similar statement of worship: "Our Father in heaven, hallowed be your name" (Matthew 6:9). As a kind father wants to care for his children, God delights to listen to our requests, but the human heart is prone to *use* God rather than adore him. If we're not careful, we start looking to God like he's a genie who should grant our wishes rather than a Savior and best friend. To guard against this, Jesus teaches us to begin our prayer with a simple statement of adoration. It's not a formula, as if we *must* pray like this or God won't listen. However, it's wise to bathe our prayers in praise—to remind our hearts of the goodness and greatness of the One we're praying to. The world wants to water down your worship, but starting with adoration reorients your heart, mind, and soul toward the Lord.

So, as you begin journaling, write down a few things you're thankful for. It might be something about God himself: "Lord, thank you for being patient with me. Thank you for being holy. I'm grateful that you're powerful and hold all things together." It might be something God has done in your life: "Lord, thank you for guiding me through a tough season. God, thank you for blessing my spouse at work yesterday. Thank you for providing enough to make rent. Thank you for sunshine today." Focusing on God's character and actions prompts gratitude. We often think of thankfulness as a trite value—something that's nice but not necessary. Yet it's powerful. When you pause to recognize the Lord's work in your life and the lives of those around you, it moves you from grumbling to gratefulness.

The benefit of writing out your gratitude every day is that you will begin to accrue a living record of God's faithfulness. Gratitude, like anything, compounds over time. Every time you choose to give thanks and adore God, you're resisting the temptation to forget his kindness. Jadedness is a sign of forgetfulness. Guard your heart against cynicism. Choose adoration. The Lord is with you, and he is faithful.

2. Intercession: Pray for Others

The second line of the Lord's Prayer is "Your kingdom come, your will be done, on earth as it is in heaven" (verse 10). Following adoration, I dedicate time to pray for others—family, friends, and broader community needs. I've found that this habit of praying for others before myself aligns my heart more with God's. To intercede for others not only imitates the Lord's Prayer but also reflects what Jesus is doing *right now*. It's mind-blowing, but Scripture teaches that "Christ Jesus . . . is at the right hand of God and is also interceding for us" (Romans 8:34). Every breath you take and moment you're alive is covered by the prayers of Jesus.

Just as Jesus prays over you, he calls you to pray over others. Our regular prayer should be "Lord, may your kingdom come and your will be done in the life of this person. May it be in their life as it is in heaven."

Interceding for others extends our prayers beyond personal desires to the needs and well-being of others. It sets our sights on God's kingdom and reminds us we are part of *his* story.

3. Supplication: Make Personal Requests to God

The next few lines of the Lord's Prayer are "Give us today our daily bread. And forgive us our debts, as we also have forgiven our debtors. And lead us not into temptation, but deliver us from the evil one" (Matthew 6:11–13). There's a lot to unpack here, but for starters, notice that this section is focused on personal requests to God. If one error is to approach God as a vending machine whose sole purpose is to satisfy our whims, the opposite mistake is to assume God is put off by our needs. God is not a CEO who gets annoyed when you knock on his door. On the contrary, Scripture encourages us to make requests with boldness and persistence:

> I say to you: Ask and it will be given to you; seek and you will find; knock and the door will be opened to you. For everyone who asks receives; the one who seeks finds; and to the one who knocks, the door will be opened. (Luke 11:9–10)

True, God doesn't give us everything we want in the timing we prefer. However, even when he says no, he's teaching us to become more dependent. He's training us to trust him. As you journal, pour out your needs to God. Don't hold back. Not only can God handle your needs, but he is also thrilled to provide for you. When you write down your requests, it's relieving, a symbolic way of surrendering your life into his hands. A way to lay down your worries and reaffirm your reliance on him.

4. Reflection: Memorize Scripture

The Lord's Prayer ends with the declaration "Yours is the kingdom and the power and the glory forever. Amen."[3] It's a powerful reminder of God's sovereignty and reinforces the truths of his Word. Memorizing Scripture cements these truths in our minds and hearts. That's why, to close each session, I focus on a memory verse. As it says in Psalm 1:1–3,

> Blessed is the one . . .
> whose delight is in the law of the LORD,
>   and who meditates on his law day and night.
> That person is like a tree planted by streams of water,
>   which yields its fruit in season
> and whose leaf does not wither—
>   whatever they do prospers.

As you cultivate godly ambition and get busy fulfilling your calling, you'll need the wisdom of God's Word. I have friends who have memorized lengthy portions of Scripture, and if that's your goal, well done. Personally, I prefer to set smaller goals and focus on one short verse at a time. Do whatever works best for you. The point is to not just get into God's Word but let God's Word get into you.

A LIFE WELL-LIVED

Imagine the potential of a life where ambition is fueled not by self-interest but by a commitment to serve and uplift others in accordance with God's plan. This life is possible through prayer. It ensures our goals are not just good for us but also good for the world. As we commit our plans to God in prayer, we open ourselves to his redirection, timing, and provision.

Beware of the lie that says you can channel your own ambition and pave your own way. Yes, the Lord has gifted and called you, but don't ever be ashamed to rely on him. To cling to his promises. To seek his direction. To intercede for others.

MY PRAYER FOR YOU

If you've spent any time in Christian circles, you've likely heard this beautiful promise: "Do not be anxious about anything, but in every situation, by prayer and petition, with thanksgiving, present your requests to God. And the peace of God, which transcends all understanding, will guard your hearts and your minds in Christ Jesus" (Philippians 4:6–7).

Familiar as this passage may be, don't glaze over this life-changing truth. As someone who's hustled his heart out, slipping into exhaustion and disorientation, I'm here to remind you that a life of prayer—a life of waiting on God—is the path to peace. Yes, work hard. Get after it. Hustle. But underneath all that activity, your soul is meant to be steady, resilient, and nourished.

Your greatest potential will never be realized through solo effort. Only when you partner with your King, communing with him often, will you bear the fruit you are created to produce. It feels fitting to end this chapter with a prayer for *you*, as you continue to cultivate godly ambition.

Father, thank you for my friend, who has chosen to journey through this book. I pray these pages will fuel their ambition—not in a self-serving way but in a kingdom-minded way.

Lord, as you taught us to pray, use my friend to bring about your will and kingdom on earth as it is in heaven. Strengthen their arms to carry those who can no longer stand. Give them clear sight to see what you're up to in the world. Renew their mind so that they might understand your Word. And quicken their

feet to put it into action to bring hope and light to a hurting world.

As they seek you in prayer, meet with them, Father. Make your presence known, increase their desire to spend time with you, and help them keep in step with your Spirit.

Bless them and keep them, Lord. Fill them with joy as they seek your presence. Protect them from the enemy. And shield them with your mighty hand.

As they learn to use their time, talent, and treasure for your glory, fill them with awe at the wonders you work in and through them.

In Jesus's name, amen.

11

Prepare for Setbacks

"Your YouTube channel will be deleted in seven days."

My heart dropped.

I reread the message. Surely this was a mistake.

A few days earlier, I'd received two emails informing me of copyright strikes against me. These weren't frivolous claims. They were lodged by a team representing a well-known celebrity podcaster—a figure whose episodes I had reacted to multiple times on my channel. Our team always strives to adhere to copyright law, to avoid situations like this, but now we were being challenged. Everything was up in the air.

YouTube is like baseball: three strikes and you're out. We already had two, and I felt my livelihood hanging in the balance. Once your channel is deleted, it's gone forever. I reflected on how much we'd invested in the channel—late nights editing, meticulously planning each segment, engaging with fans, and adapting to the ever-changing algorithms of YouTube. The stakes were incredibly high not just for me but for my four full-time employees, two part-time employees, and a handful of contractors whose families all depended on the livelihood provided by our channel.

If you haven't noticed, life throws curveballs. I'm sure you have your version of this story, when expectations crumbled in seconds, leaving you shell-shocked and unsure what to do. We all have these moments when our dreams are suddenly in danger of extinction. Maybe you got fired. Or the love of your life left you. Maybe your business never got off the ground, or it left you wallowing in debt. Perhaps you had your heart set on a career that never panned out. You didn't get into med school. You couldn't get traction on your channel. An injury ended your athletic career. As the saying goes, the only certain thing in life is uncertainty. As terrifying as it was to have my YouTube channel hanging in the balance, it wasn't my first collision with a crisis. There was a time I decided to quit my ministry job, not sure if I'd be able to pay rent. In 2017, my music label failed, and I had to start over. During the pandemic in 2020, the momentum I'd built around my music career instantly died. I didn't see any of these setbacks coming, and when they did, they knocked the wind out of me, mentally and emotionally.

As much as we all wish our dreams would unfold without a wrinkle, this isn't real life. No matter what you're building for the kingdom, setbacks will come. Some of your aspirations will die in front of your eyes. Projects will take longer than expected. Some will take off quickly, then fizzle out. The question is not *if* life will knock you down (because it will) but how to respond when it does. I want to share some key lessons I've learned through my own setbacks so you can prepare for yours.

DETOURS AND DELAYS

Setbacks are disorienting. In those moments, it's tempting to question God's goodness (or our own wisdom). We wonder whether we've strayed from his will. Or whether this is some kind of punishment. Or fill in the blank. Why does God allow detours and delays—and even the death of some dreams?

Most of the time, I don't know. That's the honest answer. God, in his wisdom, lets us fail. But here's what I do know: In God's economy, no experience—however painful—is wasted. *Ever.* During my copyright fiasco, did I enjoy reaching out to an attorney and wading through the particulars of digital media law? No, it was excruciating. Did I enjoy the brutally honest conversations with my team about the uncertainty of their future employment? Not at all. I love those guys and felt ashamed I might let them down. Did I enjoy the look on my wife's face when I broke the news? Though she supported me and helped me brainstorm, it broke my heart to see her stressed and anxious.

Yet as difficult as it was, looking back, I see God's unmistakable hand. I can't tell you *why* it happened, but I can tell you *what* happened in me. For the first time since my channel took off, I realized how fragile my business (and my life) truly is. It humbled me to realize that what took me ten years to build could collapse in a single day. When faced with that dismal reality, I found myself clinging to God's promises more than ever before.

PRINCIPLES FOR WEATHERING SETBACKS

While there's no silver bullet to eliminate setbacks, I've learned several principles along the way to help me navigate these harrowing seasons. I share them with you here because, one day—perhaps even soon—the phone call will come. The dreaded email will land in your inbox. The client will back out. Let's get you ready for that moment.

Principle 1: Know That Setbacks Build Character

God cares more about your character than your success. When we walk through fire, it refines us. As C. S. Lewis famously said, "God whispers to us in our pleasures, speaks in our conscience, but shouts in our pains: it is His megaphone to rouse a deaf world."[1]

The problem is, it's uncomfortable. No one wants to learn through pain. We want to succeed, not struggle. However, sometimes setbacks are a mysterious gift God allows in our lives. "We also glory in our sufferings, because we know that suffering produces perseverance; perseverance, character; and character, hope. And hope does not put us to shame, because God's love has been poured out into our hearts through the Holy Spirit, who has been given to us" (Romans 5:3–5). This passage suggests that our struggles, while daunting, have *purpose*—they cultivate virtues like perseverance, character, and hope.

When everything's going well—business is booming, our family is healthy, and our community is strong—it's easy to assume we're on the right track. God graciously grants us seasons of ease and comfort, but he's also willing to challenge us to increase our resilience and reliance on him. This principle—that setbacks build character—is built into every aspect of life, as described by Greg Lukianoff and Jonathan Haidt:

> Human beings *need* physical and mental challenges and stressors or we deteriorate. For example, muscles and joints need stressors to develop properly. Too much rest causes muscles to atrophy, joints to lose range of motion, heart and lung function to

decline, and blood clots to form. Without the challenges imposed by gravity, astronauts develop muscle weakness and joint degeneration.[2]

Setbacks are an inevitable part of the human experience, and whether it's personal loss, professional failures, or unforeseen crises, these moments refine us. It sounds cliché, but lean into this truth: God does some of his best work in the valley. Without this training, you would never be able to climb the mountain. Looking back, I'm now thankful for the low points in my entrepreneurial journey—those times I reached my limit and didn't know where to turn. As I cried out to God, he met me in the wilderness. And I emerged a different person.

When setbacks come, ask yourself, *Lord, what do you want me to learn in this season?* Relentlessly ask that question. God is faithful; he will show you not only what to do but also who he's calling you to become.

Principle 2: Remember That Joy Is Possible

When dreams get dashed or delayed, it's natural to despair or give in to discouragement. I encourage you to feel these emotions. Give them a voice—just don't let them take over. To keep my soul buoyant when it feels like I'm drowning, I often return to this verse: "We are hard pressed on every side, but not crushed; perplexed, but not in despair" (2 Corinthians 4:8). As followers of Jesus, we're free to bring our full lament before God. At the same time, we don't grieve as those without hope. Why? Because God never abandons his children in their hour of need. He promises to never leave you or forsake you (Hebrews 13:5).

Not only can we avoid despair, but we can also embrace hope. This sounds counterintuitive to the world: Why would you rejoice when life seems to be working against you? "Consider it pure joy, my brothers and sisters, whenever you face trials of many kinds, because you know that the testing of your faith produces perseverance. Let perseverance finish its work so that you may be mature and complete, not lacking anything" (James 1:2–4).

This passage became a beacon in the tumultuous days following the copyright strikes. I had a choice between fear and joy. I know I didn't do this perfectly, but to the best of my ability, I tried to model joy to my family, my team, and my fans. Knowing my channel might be deleted, I had to keep my audience updated day by day. Though I stressed the urgency of the situation and asked them to pray, I also emphasized that whatever the outcome, God is good. Was anxiety welling up within me? Absolutely. Still, I experienced joy in that season. When all options seem like dead ends, you get a front-row seat to God's deliverance. Even in the valley, you can rejoice.

Think about the setbacks you've experienced—perhaps you're in the middle of one right now. What if these trials aren't divine abandonments but divine appointments? What if God has led you here because he loves you? What if you will emerge from this more confident in God's faithfulness? This isn't wishful thinking; it's the way of Jesus. The same God who made a highway through the wilderness, who split the Red Sea to save his people, will make a way for you. There will be moments when water and food seem scarce, when enemies surround, when you feel lost and aimless in a barren wasteland. But the Lord is with you. He's by your side.

So, while you wander, choose joy.

Principle 3: Get Busy

Sometimes in our desire to trust God, we grow passive. We expect him to do the heavy lifting, which in some cases is the only option. At times when our strength is sapped, we just need deliverance. This is how salvation works: We bring nothing and God provides everything. However, God also desires to partner with you—to help you take steps rather than take them for you. To let you struggle through a new process so you learn. He invites you to be proactive, not just passive.

Once I received the dismal news about my channel, one of my first decisions was to point my audience toward Patreon, an online community where fans can financially support their favorite creators and artists. If YouTube shut me down, I would need other income streams. This decision was not a lack of faith; it was a strategic move that took seriously the possibility of losing a large portion of my income. As I said in the last chapter, the practical and spiritual elements of life weave together. It's not "more spiritual" to pray without action. When things go haywire, bathe them in prayer, make a plan, and then act wisely. In my case, I had seven days to figure it out. Hopefully you'll have more time, but life comes at you fast, so you may have to make a split-second decision.

Initially, I enlisted the help of a lawyer and filed counter notifications. This escalated the situation, requiring the firm that issued the strikes to either drop the claims or pursue them in federal court. Rather than wait for the chips to fall, I took the initiative to defend my livelihood. There will be times when the right thing to do is to stand up for yourself. Again, God's providence includes partnering with you. Don't be afraid to take bold action when the time is right.

As setbacks come, regroup and review. Take a moment to analyze your situation. From there, it's time to act. God has given you this responsibility, so steward it. The good news is, he doesn't expect you to figure it out alone.

Principle 4: Seek Wisdom and Counsel

It's tempting to try to navigate setbacks alone. Resist this urge. In our culture of achievement, where everyone poses like they have it all together, it can feel embarrassing to admit we've hit a roadblock. It's vulnerable to send up a smoke signal to say, "Help! I need help!" Yet God has placed people in your life—friends, mentors, colleagues, family, whomever—to help guide you through tough moments.

Without the help of others, I don't know that my YouTube channel would have survived. "Without counsel plans fail, but with many advisers they succeed" (Proverbs 15:22, ESV). Here's how it went down. First, I contacted a legal expert well-versed in digital copyright law. He gave me sound advice about how to navigate the claims against me. I also reached out to experienced peers, who gave practical advice and moral support. Their collective wisdom led us to pivot our strategy, helping us make wise decisions instead of reacting out of fear or anger. With these friends around me, it felt like a group effort. The sense that I wasn't alone provided peace and steadied my nerves.

Perhaps the greatest breakthrough came when a mutual friend who understood the gravity of the situation informed the celebrity podcaster of the strikes. The podcaster was quick to respond, expressing his surprise and concern. He assured me that he would personally investigate the matter. Almost instantly, all four strikes were lifted, and the imminent threat to my channel was averted. It turned out the strikes had been issued by an overzealous legal team without his authorization.

I owe this rapid resolution to a friend who was willing to go to bat for me. God providentially orchestrates the relationships in our lives. In your darkest hour, he'll provide someone to advocate for you, guide you, and support you. Your role is to reach out, even when it's uncomfortable. For instance, I wrestled with whether I should bother this friend. I also worried about making a poor first impression on the well-known podcaster. In the end, everyone was helpful and no harm was done.

Principle 5: Maintain Integrity

In the midst of this copyright scare, the temptation to lash out was strong. I wanted to fight back, perhaps even bend the rules to secure a quick solution. Whenever we've been wronged, retribution is attractive. Shortcuts promise a quick fix. A little compromise here and there won't hurt, right? It's a slippery slope.

Yet this experience reinforced the value of integrity. "The integrity of the upright guides them, but the crookedness of the treacherous destroys them" (Proverbs 11:3, ESV). By choosing to respond legally and ethically, maintaining transparency with my team and my audience, I preserved my channel's reputation and, more importantly, my heart. It might feel good to strike back in a dishonest or deceptive way, but as Scripture warns, it leads to destruction. Staying calm, seeking peaceful solutions, and taking decisive action honor God.

At first, it may seem easier to fudge the numbers on your tax return to avoid the hard reality that your business is struggling. Or to highlight an adversary's flaws after they drag your name through the mud. Or to settle for mediocre product standards because it boosts the bottom line. But in the end, the truth wins out. Temporary compromise creates long-term complication. On the flip side, integrity stings up front, but over time, it creates a life of peace and flourishing. Serious problems rarely have instant solutions. Rather than ignore the issue, face it head-on. If you refuse to budge on your convictions, it's an opportunity to watch God provide for you. His solutions are superior anyway, so why not let him show up?

Where are you tempted to compromise? How have you cut corners in the past, and how can you resolve to make better, God-honoring decisions? Has there been a time you chose integrity, and though it seemed impractical at the time, you're thankful you embraced God's way? Resolve now to face setbacks with integrity in place. It's one of the few things no one can take from you. It's a souvenir you want to carry out of every trial.

Principle 6: Embrace the Sovereignty of God

As the deadline for potentially losing my channel approached, I found myself panicking. How could years of hard work be threatened so suddenly? *Lord, why would you allow this to happen?* As my anxiety grew, my mind drifted to Job, a man who lost everything he cared about. In the midst of unthinkable loss, he declared, "The LORD gave, and the LORD has taken away; blessed be the name of the LORD" (1:21, ESV). Not an easy thing to pray. Yet I knew these words were my marching orders, no matter what happened. The more I internalized this truth—*God gives and takes away; blessed be his name*—the more it became a lifeline. My nerves settled. Joy peeked through the storm, just enough to calm my soul.

God "works out everything in conformity with the purpose of his will" (Ephesians 1:11). What looks like a maze to us is manageable for him. He is in control. He's never surprised or outmatched. And with the wisdom of an experienced captain, he is gently steering your life into his safe harbor. This can be difficult to believe when your plans crumble around you. When a chapter abruptly ends, even though you thought the story would continue. When your job is on the line. When the economy takes a downturn, leaving your dream in ruins. But know this: God is in control. You can trust him, even when resolution seems impossible.

I'm thankful my YouTube channel survived, but there have been many other scenarios in which I've had to lay my dreams down. Things didn't work out. In the moment, it felt unbearable to pour *so much* of myself into something only to have it crash and burn. But even in these lost dreams, I've seen God's sovereign hand at work.

Take comfort in your Good Shepherd, who leads you with wisdom. As Jesus promised, "I give them eternal life, and they shall never perish; no one will snatch them out of my hand" (John 10:28). As a follower of Jesus, you can be sure your future is secure. So, take heart. The Lord holds you in his hand, and he'll never let you go.

WHEN SETBACKS ARE YOUR FAULT

How should you view a setback when you're the one who caused it? Sometimes problems happen *to* you; other times they happen *because of* you. It could be a business mistake, like miscalculating your budget or hiring the wrong person. It could be a hasty decision you later regret. Missteps slow down progress. It's painful to realize we caused a setback, but even in these unfortunate scenarios, God is at work.

My friend Timothy committed a violent crime and was sentenced to more than ten years in prison. One bad decision cost him his freedom for more than a decade. It's hard to imagine a more devastating setback—one he admits that he deserved but that still cost him dearly. Inside the confines of his cell, with every other commitment stripped from his life, Timothy signed up for various courses, investing in his personal and professional development. He established a routine that included working out, reading, and studying the Bible. Eventually, he had the opportunity to pitch a business idea to some investors, a sort of Shark Tank program for prisoners. His business idea, an environmental cleaning service aimed at high-end commercial buildings, won the contest.

It was a pivotal moment in Timothy's life. It provided him with the start-up funding to establish Quality Touch Cleaning Systems. Now he's out of prison, and his business is thriving, employing multiple staff members and managing contracts around San Diego.

Some hurdles in your path will be those you set up yourself, whether intentionally or unintentionally. But even when it's your fault, God will meet you there. What's true in Timothy's life is true in yours: You are not defined by your mistakes. From the ashes of failure, God brings new life.

CHOOSE NOW

None of us can predict when setbacks will come. All we can do is prepare our hearts for their arrival. Choose *now* to trust and honor God when things hit the fan. Ask God to build integrity into your character so that when you're tested, you can stand strong. I love God's instructions to Joshua when he installed Joshua as Israel's leader. As you read these words, make them your prayer to God:

> Be strong and very courageous. Be careful to obey all the law my servant Moses gave you; do not turn from it to the right or to the left, that you may be successful wherever you go. Keep this Book of the Law always on your lips; meditate on it day and night, so that you may be careful to do everything written in it. Then you will be prosperous and successful. Have I not commanded you? Be strong and courageous. Do not be afraid; do not be discouraged, for the LORD your God will be with you wherever you go. (Joshua 1:7–9)

Friend, God is with you. There's no better news than that. Your setbacks are merely a stage for his sovereignty. Your failures are an opportunity to grow in humility and wisdom. Nothing can derail God's plans for you. Whether the Lord gives or takes away, I pray you find the strength to say, "Blessed be the name of the Lord."

Conclusion

As we conclude this journey, I hope you're more convinced you've been put here by God for a purpose. I hope you're eager to steward your ambitions for the kingdom. And I pray you're clearer about your calling. I've given you much to think about; now it's time to take action. In these final pages, my goal is to give you some final advice to help you use your time, talent, and treasure to love God and make him known.

So, here are ten principles to help you move forward. They're not linear, as if you must follow them in a particular order. Nor should you feel the burden to tackle all of them at once. As you read through the list, ask God to highlight one or two. I've also included a scripture and a reflection question with each principle to help you internalize and apply it.

I pray these ten principles stir up godly ambition within you.

1. Work Diligently unto the Lord

> Whatever you do, work at it with all your heart,
> as working for the Lord, not for human masters.
> —Colossians 3:23

It's not uncommon to hear employers complain that "no one wants to work these days." While probably overstated, this comment still holds a kernel of truth. Your work ethic is one of the primary ways to reflect Jesus and serve the world. In chapter 4, "Master the Fundamentals," I talked about the temptation to take shortcuts now—especially if you're unhappy or bored at work—to reach a more desirable destination in the future.

I encourage you to resist this temptation. Roll up your sleeves, and give your all as an act of service unto God. By ignoring the status quo and serving with your whole self, you'll not only preserve your integrity but also earn the respect of your employers (which is likely to open doors down the road). Even if you're in a thankless job, working under an unappreciative supervisor, the type of character you build in this season will follow you forever. Work today to become the person you want to be tomorrow.

Reflection question: Have you been serving half-heartedly in any areas, and if so, how is God inviting you to give your all?

2. TEST YOUR AMBITIONS, BUT TAKE THEM SERIOUSLY

> Search me, God, and know my heart;
>   test me and know my anxious thoughts.
> See if there is any offensive way in me,
>   and lead me in the way everlasting.
> —PSALM 139:23–24

I hope it's clear by now that ambition does not have to be a dirty word. It's always wise to test our desires, submitting them to God and our community, but if the Spirit is stirring something in your heart, honor that. Investigate it. Sometimes our ambitions are like threads we pull—not knowing exactly where they'll lead but being willing to find out.

Christians like to criticize the mantra "Follow your heart" because we're all prone to sin. Though your heart *can* mislead you (Jeremiah 17:9), as a follower of Jesus, you are a new creation who is capable of hearing his voice (John 10:27). God's voice isn't always audible; sometimes you'll hear it in Scripture, through the counsel of others, and through inner whispers, promptings, and desires.

The difference between godly and selfish ambition can be subtle. So, don't follow your heart blindly, but don't ignore it either.

Reflection question: What is one ambition or goal that captures your imagination? How can you bring it before God and others to test whether or not you should pursue it?

3. Seek Out a Mentor

Plans fail for lack of counsel,
> but with many advisers they succeed.
> —Proverbs 15:22

In chapter 9, "Connect to Community," I shared about a few people who have mentored me through the years. Sometimes this was informal—just casual conversations at church. Other times it was more intentional, like meeting in someone's home for a Bible study or seeking to learn from a more mature married couple.

Don't fall into the common trap of self-pity because it seems like no one wants to pour into you. Meaningful relationships don't usually fall into your lap—you have to seek them out. Instead of expecting wisdom to find you, go find wisdom.

> My son, if you accept my words
>   and store up my commands within you,
> turning your ear to wisdom
>   and applying your heart to understanding—
> indeed, if you call out for insight
>   and cry aloud for understanding,
> and if you look for it as for silver
>   and search for it as for hidden treasure,
> then you will understand the fear of the Lord
>   and find the knowledge of God. (Proverbs 2:1–5)

You cannot cultivate godly ambition alone. You need more seasoned believers by your side, cheering you on, holding you accountable, and sharing from their experience. I've been saved from *so much* heartache and wasted time and so many foolish decisions by heeding the counsel of mentors. I want the same for you.

Reflection question: Think of someone in your life who could potentially mentor you. How can you initiate a conversation with them this week?

4. Commit (or Recommit) to a Local Church

> Let us consider how we may spur one another on toward love and good deeds, not giving up meeting together, as some are in the habit of doing, but encouraging one another.
>
> —Hebrews 10:24–25

Godly ambition is forged in the context of a church community. This requires us to surrender a portion of our autonomy (in terms of time and attention), but in return, we receive the gift of belonging in God's family. According to Oliver Burkeman, community is a price worth paying:

> The question is, What kind of freedom do we really want when it comes to time? On the one hand, there's the culturally celebrated goal of individual time sovereignty—the freedom to set your own schedule, to make your own choices, to be *free from* other people's intrusions into your precious four thousand weeks. On the other hand, there's the profound sense of meaning that comes from being willing to fall in with the rhythms of the rest of the world: to be *free to* engage in all the worthwhile collaborative endeavors that require at least some sacrifice of your sole control over what you do and when.[1]

Burkeman doesn't profess to be a Christian, but he articulates so well the satisfaction that comes from integrating into a church. As I discussed in chapter 9, the church is where much of your calling will be discerned and affirmed. What a gift to serve alongside others who love Jesus—to pour into them and be poured into.

If you've been avoiding church for a while (perhaps for understandable reasons), consider what it might look like to return, even if you need to find a new church. I don't pretend to know the details of your situation or the pain you've experienced, but know that God's heart is to lead you back to a safe place. There are shepherds, and whole communities, who will know and love you fully.

Reflection question: If you currently belong to a local church, what is one way you can participate or serve in this season? What ministry, friendship, or opportunity will allow you to bless others with your gifts?

5. IDENTIFY ONE SKILL TO GROW IN OR ONE NEW SKILL TO ACQUIRE

> We have different gifts, according to the grace given to each of us.
> —ROMANS 12:6

In chapter 5, "Stack Your Talents," I encouraged you to find your formula—your distinctive combination of gifts that no one else can replicate. This unicorn skill set is how God has wired you, and it's your unique contribution to his kingdom.

As you gain clarity about your calling, maybe you'd like to grow more proficient in a certain ability. You have ambition to do something, but you lack the knowledge or skill to accomplish it. Perhaps this is a season to invest in that skill. Consider what it will require in terms of time, money, and other resources. Audit the season you're in to discern whether you can invest what it will take.

As a reminder, you can become more proficient at a lot of things with just twenty hours of intentional practice. Acquiring a new skill can feel daunting, but don't overthink it. After twenty hours, you're *slightly* better than when you started, and that's a win. Remember my mantra: "Incremental adjustments lead to monumental advancements." Your efforts will compound if you stick with them for the long haul.

Reflection question: What is one existing skill you want to grow in or one new skill you want to acquire? Think about when, where, and how often you'll invest in this skill. Make a plan, and stick with it.

6. Talk with Someone You Trust About Your Ambitions

> Encourage one another and build each other up.
> —1 Thessalonians 5:11

As I've shared throughout this book, you don't have to sift through your ambitions alone. One of my favorite habits is to ask someone I trust to process with me. It doesn't have to be a mentor (although that works too)—just someone who knows you deeply and loves you. If it feels awkward to schedule a conversation about yourself, frame it like this: "Hey, I've been thinking about God's call on my life, and I'd love to process that with you. Would you be willing to meet up and share your wisdom with me?" As a starting point, talk through the three questions covered in chapter 3:

1. What do I love doing? (passion)
2. How do my gifts meet the world's needs? (mission)
3. What can I get paid to do? (vocation)

If the person knows your story well, ask them to help you "follow the favor" in your life. Meaning, look for patterns of God's blessing on your efforts. What activities or ministries have been the most fruitful? Where do people seem genuinely helped by you? Where do you sense God's pleasure and approval in your life? Talking with another person may reveal patterns you haven't thought about.

Reflection question: As you sift through your ambitions and seek God's calling, whom do you trust to invite into your discernment process?

7. Introduce Yourself to Someone You Look Up To

> One who loves a pure heart and who speaks with grace
> will have the king for a friend.
> —Proverbs 22:11

It can be intimidating to approach someone you respect, whether you admire their professional accomplishments, character, or knowledge. In chapter 8, "Collaborate with Others," I encouraged you to be a "relentless initiator." The ability to form new connections is a vital soft skill that will help you grow and build your network. Every time you branch out, it not only benefits you but also broadens your bandwidth, allowing you to bless more people.

If you tend to be timid or introverted, I highly recommend you implement this step. Tackling tasks we feel insecure about is a healthy discipline. It forces us to rely on God, and when we emerge on the other side, we're thankful we took the leap.

If you have a mutual connection, ask for a warm introduction. That's always preferred. If not, send a brief DM or email introducing yourself, expressing appreciation for who the person is and what they do and asking if they're willing to connect.

Reflection question: Who is someone you deeply respect and would feel a little nervous to talk to? Reach out to them today.

8. Journal Your Prayers for Seven Days

Great are the works of the LORD;
> they are pondered by all who delight in them.
> —PSALM 111:2

As I shared in chapter 10, "Pray Boldly," the habit of journaling my prayers has sustained me through the ups and downs of my personal life and career. Prayer journaling creates a written record of God's answers to your prayers. It slows you down so you can hear your own thoughts and abide with Jesus.

I recommend setting a realistic goal: Try to journal your prayers for at least seven days. Anyone can try something for one week. If you decide to keep going—wonderful. And don't get hung up on how long you spend journaling each day. If it's five minutes, that works. If you have more time to invest, take advantage of it. What I *do* recommend is keeping the time and place consistent over those seven days. If it's helpful, set an alarm to remind yourself.

As I've mentioned before, I created a prayer journal that is available at blessgod.shop (although any journal will do). If you're looking for guidance on what to pray and write about, follow these four simple steps:

1. **Adoration:** Write a few sentences about the character or work of God. How has he shown up for you? Why is he worthy of praise?

2. **Intercession:** Write down a few prayer requests for people in your life or burdens the Lord has placed on your heart. Who in your life needs to experience God in this season? Does someone need healing, forgiveness, or hope? Is there a cause that's burdening your heart—a need for justice, forgiveness, or tangible aid?
3. **Supplication:** Write out some of your personal prayer requests. Where are you anxious, hopeful, sad, or expectant? Pour out your heart to God, believing that he cares for you and will answer according to his wisdom and timing.
4. **Memorization of scripture:** Write out a short memory verse that you'd like to internalize in this season. Say it out loud as you write it. Commit to the same verse for one full week so that by the end, you can recite it from memory.

Reflection question: When and where will you journal for the next seven days? How do you anticipate this practice will impact your ambition?

9. Choose an Identity Anchor Verse

I have hidden your word in my heart
that I might not sin against you.
—Psalm 119:11

It's easy to lose ourselves in ambition, which is why it's so important to anchor our identities in Christ. As I shared in chapter 2, "Identity: Know Who You Are," one of the most effective ways to rehearse your God-given identity is to memorize scripture. Every part of God's Word is "living and active" (Hebrews 4:12, ESV). "All Scripture is God-breathed and is useful for teaching, rebuking, correcting and training in righteousness, so that the servant of God may be thoroughly equipped for every good work" (2 Timothy 3:16–17). So, you can't go wrong in choosing a verse or passage. Still, here are a few pointers to get you going.

When choosing a verse, look for themes in your life. Is there a verse that's played a significant role in your life? An attribute of God you've always admired? A promise that's sustained you in difficult times? Have particular words of Jesus always moved you? Start there. Ask the Holy Spirit to guide your search.

I find it helpful to write the scripture down on a note card or sticky note, then place it where I see it every day—on the bathroom mirror, beside my bed, or on my car dashboard. You could even make it your phone's lock screen or background.

Reflection question: What is a major theme in Scripture that stands out to you? How has this theme woven its way through your life?

10. Identify and Eliminate One Distraction from Your Life

> Let your eyes look straight ahead;
>   fix your gaze directly before you.
> Give careful thought to the paths for your feet
>   and be steadfast in all your ways.
> Do not turn to the right or the left;
>   keep your foot from evil.
>
> —Proverbs 4:25–27

It's a bit cliché to talk about distraction these days, yet it's one of the greatest obstacles to godly ambition. We're bombarded with information, entertainment, and endless options for how to spend our time. Quite honestly, I'm not sure it's possible to tune out *all* distraction. But it's helpful to start somewhere. In chapter 7, "Defeat Distraction," I gave the following five suggestions:

1. **Set a specific limit on media consumption:** Create a plan that outlines how often you will stream shows, listen to podcasts, or (dare I say it) watch YouTube.
2. **Create before consuming:** Establish a daily rhythm in which you produce before you consume. It could be as simple as "I will read my Bible and write in my prayer journal before I check my phone." If you're an artist or creative, rather than checking in on what everyone else is doing, make something first.
3. **Choose a few daily non-negotiables:** Pick two or three simple actions you will carry out every single day that will help you accomplish your goals. No matter what, do these things every day for a set period of time.
4. **Optimize your environment for deep work:** Clear your workspace of distractions, including your phone. Instead of bringing a tablet or laptop to meetings, bring a notepad and pen.
5. **Gamify your goals:** Make it more fun to hit your benchmarks by setting up a simple reward system. It doesn't have to be extravagant; for example, one person I know treats himself to a Topo Chico every time he finishes a run. It's his favorite drink, and this tiny boost in motivation gets him out the door and jogging. Figure out what will motivate you, then work it into your routine.

As you pray through this list, discerning your next step, know that I have been praying for you. I'm so thankful God is calling you, here and now, to impact the world with your unique gifts. My sincere hope is that this book has thrown logs on the fire of your ambition.

OCCUPY TILL I COME

In Luke 19, Jesus tells a story about a man who is going on a journey, but before he departs, he entrusts his servants with resources and commands them to be good stewards of these until he returns. In the King James Version, the master says, "Occupy till I come" (verse 13). I love that phrase. To me, the concept of "occupying" is about being diligent, proactive, and faithful in our work, knowing we will each have to give an account.

In Matthew's version of this story, when the master eventually returns home and settles accounts with each servant, he says to those who stewarded his resources well, "Well done, good and faithful servant! You have been faithful with a few things; I will put you in charge of many things. Come and share your master's happiness!" (25:21).

Though some days it feels a million miles away, a day is coming when you will be face-to-face with Jesus—when you will have an opportunity to look into his eyes and hear those words of affirmation: "Well done." Can you picture that moment? Do you long for it? You might feel like there isn't much in your hands, but even so, God has entrusted *you* with those things. Be faithful with them.

The wonderful truth about God is that we don't serve him to earn his love; we serve him because we are *already* loved. Never reverse this. In the world, approval has to be earned, and even when you pull it off, you're perpetually afraid of losing it. Not so with Jesus. In him, you are fully known and fully loved. Your merit comes not from what you do but from what he has done through his life, death, and resurrection. His acceptance of you is not dependent on your success, appearance, or giftedness. Isn't that comforting?

Let grace fuel your ambition. Discover the joy of running hard after the goals ahead, in the freedom of being a beloved son or daughter of God. Your heavenly Father is cheering you on. So am I.

Acknowledgments

First and foremost, I want to thank my Lord and Savior Jesus Christ. Without his grace, mercy, and intervention, none of this would have been possible. He rescued me, reconciled me with the Father, and completely altered the trajectory of my life. I was once a kid from Baku, a refugee with baggage, brokenness, and ambition aimed in all the wrong directions. But God stepped in. He gave me purpose, discipline, and above all, himself. This book is an offering back to him. May it serve his kingdom.

To my incredible wife, Monette Karaoglanov, thank you for being my rock. Your quiet strength, steady faith, and constant encouragement have sustained me through every creative block and every crazy idea I've chased. Thank you for encouraging me to put in my two-weeks notice over ten years ago. You've been faithful through the highs and the lows. This journey hasn't always been easy, but you've stood beside me with grace, grit, and God's love. I love you more than words can say.

To my mom, your resilience taught me what it means to persevere. You sacrificed much, so I could have a better life. I see that now. I honor your strength and the seeds of faith you planted, even when the soil was hard.

To my dad, thank you for sparking the flame of entrepreneurship in me. You showed me what it looked like to be industrious and planted in me the instinct to take risks, think creatively, and build something from nothing. God has redeemed that legacy and for that, I'm grateful.

ACKNOWLEDGMENTS

To my son, Levi, your questions stretch me in all the best ways. You remind me to stay curious, sharp, and humble. Never stop asking questions, son. The kingdom belongs to those who seek truth.

To my daughter, Zoe, your name means "life," and you embody the life Jesus came to offer us. You bring joy into every room, and your presence is a constant reminder that God gives good gifts. May you grow to understand just how loved you are in Christ.

To Zach Sperrazzo, thank you for believing in this project and for riding shotgun on this wild journey. Your friendship, input, and support have meant more than you know. You helped breathe wind into the sails of this book.

To Pastor Jeff Moors at Rhythm Church, thank you for coming alongside me when I was transitioning from doing music exclusively. Your encouragement helped me move forward with confidence and clarity during a pivotal season.

To Jason Broome, thank you for mentoring me when I was still trying to find my way. Your wisdom, feedback, and guidance through the early writing process were invaluable. You helped me sharpen the message without compromising the mission.

To Esther Fedorkevich, thank you for championing this project and making it happen. Your belief in the vision gave it legs. Thank you for your diligence, tenacity, and kingdom mindset.

To Will Anderson—this whole thing might not have happened without that one cold DM on Instagram. Thank you for taking a chance on me. Your editing brought clarity, rhythm, and power to these pages. You've been more than an editor; you've been a creative partner.

To the entire team that contributed behind the scenes, thank you. Every email, deadline, and prayer made a difference. Thank you for helping me steward this assignment well.

And finally, to the readers—this book was written for you. If it fuels your godly ambition, points you to Jesus, and reminds you that excellence and faith can coexist, then it has done its job. I pray this book throws logs on the fire of your calling. Let's go build something that blesses God.

Notes

INTRODUCTION

1. Charles Dickens, *A Tale of Two Cities* (James Nisbet, 1902), 3.
2. Adobe Acrobat Team, "Fast-Forward—Comparing a 1980s Supercomputer to the Modern Smartphone," *Adobe Blog*, November 8, 2022, https://blog.adobe.com/en/publish/2022/11/08/fast-forward-comparing-1980s-supercomputer-to-modern-smartphone.
3. Veera Korhonen, "Educational Attainment Distribution in the United States from 1960 to 2022," Statista, August 22, 2024, www.statista.com/statistics/184260/educational-attainment-in-the-us.
4. "Video Streaming Services in the US—Number of Businesses," IBISWorld, updated June 18, 2024, www.ibisworld.com/industry-statistics/number-of-businesses/video-streaming-services-united-states/.
5. "About Spotify," Spotify, accessed December 26, 2024, https://newsroom.spotify.com/company-info.
6. Jim Zarroli, "'Deaths of Despair' Examines the Steady Erosion of U.S. Working-Class Life," review of *Deaths of Despair and the Future of Capitalism*, by Anne Case and Angus Deaton, NPR, March 18, 2020, www.npr.org/2020/03/18/817687042/deaths

-of-despair-examines-the-steady-erosion-of-u-s-working-class-life.
7. Lane Gillespie, "Bankrate's 2024 Annual Emergency Savings Report," Bankrate, June 20, 2024, https://web.archive.org/web/20241230225357/https://www.bankrate.com/banking/savings/emergency-savings-report/.
8. "Overweight & Obesity Statistics," National Institute of Diabetes and Digestive and Kidney Diseases, last reviewed September 2021, www.niddk.nih.gov/health-information/health-statistics/overweight-obesity.

CHAPTER 1: IS AMBITION BAD OR GOOD?

1. Ramsey Solutions, "Gazelle Intensity: Do You Have It?," Ramsey, July 18, 2022, www.ramseysolutions.com/debt/gazelle-intensity-do-you-have-it.
2. Here is one example: "How Rich Am I?," Giving What We Can, accessed December 28, 2024, www.givingwhatwecan.org/how-rich-am-i.
3. P. T. Barnum, *Struggles and Triumphs: Or, Forty Years' Recollections of P. T. Barnum* (Hartford, Conn., 1869), 473–74, www.google.com/books/edition/Struggles_and_Triumphs/s9YydrgS3UcC.
4. Blue Letter Bible, "Strong's G2052—*eritheia*," accessed December 30, 2024, www.blueletterbible.org/lexicon/g2052/niv/mgnt/0-1/.
5. "What Was the Significance of Jesus Washing the Feet of the Disciples?," Got Questions, accessed December 30, 2024, www.gotquestions.org/Jesus-washing-feet.html.
6. Bible Hub, "5389. *philotimeomai*," accessed December 30, 2024, https://biblehub.com/greek/5389.htm.

CHAPTER 2: IDENTITY: KNOW WHO YOU ARE

1. Ruslan Karaoglanov, "Do for One," *Do for One,* Kings Dream Entertainment, 2015.
2. See, for example, "Work Your Face Off in Your 20s—Gary Vaynerchuk Motivation," Gary Vaynerchuk Fan Page, February 25, 2022, YouTube, www.youtube.com/watch?v=ies7gA2ABxI; and "'I Work 18 Hours a Day Because I Want to Win'—Gary Vaynerchuk Motivation," Gary Vaynerchuk Fan Page, November 22, 2021, YouTube, www.youtube.com/watch?v=vvV1ihn3zHs.
3. Craig Groeschel, *Altar Ego: Becoming Who God Says You Are* (Zondervan, 2013), 165.
4. James Clear, *Atomic Habits: An Easy and Proven Way to Build Good Habits and Break Bad Ones* (Avery, 2018).
5. Clear, *Atomic Habits,* 30, fig. 3.
6. Clear, *Atomic Habits,* 23–27.
7. Clear, *Atomic Habits,* 30.
8. Thomas Brennan, "Principle of Replacement," Bethlehem Church, May 11, 2018, www.bethlehemhampden.org/blog/principleofreplacement.
9. Neil T. Anderson, *Victory over the Darkness: Realize the Power of Your Identity in Christ* (Bethany House, 2013), 38–39, https://archive.org/details/victoryoverdarkn0000ande_y1a1/page/38/mode/2up?view=theater.

CHAPTER 3: CALLING: KNOW WHY YOU'RE HERE

1. "You're the Star of the Show with Main Character Syndrome," Cleveland Health Clinic, December 15, 2023, https://health.clevelandclinic.org/what-to-know-about-main-character-syndrome.

2. Jocko Willink, "Choosing Between Money and Passion at Work," excerpt from Jocko Podcast, episode 151, posted May 2, 2020, by Jocko Podcast, YouTube, 0:08–14, www.youtube.com/watch?v=k7nbtth2cSU.
3. Steve Jobs, "Steve Jobs Passion in Work," interview, May 30, 2007, posted August 2, 2011, by TheCoach, YouTube, 0:01–13, www.youtube.com/watch?v=PznJqxon4zE.
4. "Mike Rowe: Don't Pursue Your Passion. Chase Opportunity," posted August 30, 2019, by *Entrepreneur*, YouTube, 1:22–50, 2:47–50, www.youtube.com/watch?v=-KF0AN4H3U8.
5. Jerry Seinfeld, "Jerry Seinfeld Is Never Not Thinking About Comedy," interview by Howard Stern, *The Howard Stern Show*, February 24, 2023, YouTube, 2:13–18, www.youtube.com/watch?v=MaSvlSHNJEk.
6. Sean Croxton, host, *The Quote of the Day Show,* podcast, episode 982, "Les Brown: If You Do What Is Easy, Your Life Will Be Hard. But If You Do What Is Hard, Your Life Will Be Easy," August 31, 2020, 3:02–14, https://seancroxton.com/quote-of-the-day/982/.
7. *Oxford Dictionary of English,* 3rd ed. (2010), under "passion," https://archive.org/details/oxforddictionary0000unse_a2v4/page/n5/mode/2up?view=theater.

CHAPTER 5: STACK YOUR TALENTS

1. Scott Adams, "Career Advice," *Dilbert.blog,* July 20, 2007, https://dilbertblog.typepad.com/the_dilbert_blog/2007/07/career-advice.html.
2. Scott Adams, *How to Fail at Almost Everything and Still Win Big: Kind of the Story of My Life,* 2nd ed. (Scott Adams, Inc., 2023), 122.
3. Adams, "Career Advice."

4. Adams, "Career Advice."
5. Josh Kaufman, *The First 20 Hours: How to Learn Anything . . . Fast!* (Portfolio / Penguin, 2013).

CHAPTER 6: FOLLOW THE FAVOR

1. Will Heilpern, "11 Famous Products That Were Originally Intended for a Completely Different Purpose," *Business Insider*, updated September 19, 2016, www.businessinsider.com/successful-products-that-were-originally-intended-for-a-completely-different-purpose-2016-3.
2. James Clear (@JamesClear), "Inspiration comes on the twenty-fifth attempt, not the first. If you want to make something excellent, don't wait for a brilliant idea to strike," X, September 19, 2024, https://x.com/JamesClear/status/1836860439390736774.
3. James Clear, *Atomic Habits: An Easy and Proven Way to Build Good Habits and Break Bad Ones* (Avery, 2018), 17.

CHAPTER 7: DEFEAT DISTRACTION

1. Insider Intelligence Editors, "US Adults Added 1 Hour of Digital Time in 2020," *EMarketer*, January 26, 2021, www.emarketer.com/content/us-adults-added-1-hour-of-digital-time-2020.
2. "US Media Consumption (2021–2025)," Oberlo, accessed January 20, 2025, www.oberlo.com/statistics/us-media-consumption.
3. Charles Duhigg, *The Power of Habit: Why We Do What We Do in Life and Business,* 10th anniversary ed. (Random House, 2023), chap. 4.
4. Duhigg, *Power of Habit,* 109.

5. Jon Acuff, *Quitter: Closing the Gap Between Your Day Job and Your Dream Job* (Lampo, 2011).
6. Cal Newport, *Deep Work: Rules for Focused Success in a Distracted World* (Grand Central, 2016), 3.

CHAPTER 8: COLLABORATE WITH OTHERS

1. EntreLeadership, "The Dirt on Partnerships," Ramsey, November 7, 2024, www.ramseysolutions.com/business/the-dirt-on-partnerships.
2. Dave Ramsey, "The only ship that won't sail is a partnership. Business partnerships rarely work," X, May 5, 2023, https://x.com/DaveRamsey/status/1654489123728531460.
3. Marshall Hargrave, "Joint Venture (JV): What Is It, and Why Do Companies Form One?," Investopedia, updated June 14, 2024, www.investopedia.com/terms/j/jointventure.asp.

CHAPTER 9: CONNECT TO COMMUNITY

1. David C. McClelland, *The Achieving Society* (Van Nostrand, 1961); cited in Darren Hardy, *The Compound Effect* (Vanguard, 2010), 127.
2. Robert Rosenthal and Lenore Jacobson, "Pygmalion in the Classroom," *The Urban Review* 3 (1968): 16–20, https://users.wfu.edu/gemmerj/files/S23/FYS/Pygmalion-in-the-Classroom.pdf; Robert Rosenthal and Lenore Jacobson, *Pygmalion in the Classroom: Teacher Expectation and Pupils' Intellectual Development* (Crown House, 1992).
3. See, for example, Beth Nichol et al., "Exploring the Effects of Volunteering on the Social, Mental, and Physical Health and Well-Being of Volunteers: An Umbrella Review," *Voluntas* (May 4, 2023): 1–32, https://pmc.ncbi.nlm.nih.gov/articles/PMC10159229/; Terri L. Lyon and Trish Lockard, *Make a Differ-*

ence with Mental Health Activism: No Activism Degree Required—Use Your Unique Skills to Change the World (Life at the Intersection Books, 2021); Sara Konrath et al., "Motives for Volunteering Are Associated with Mortality Risk in Older Adults," *Health Psychology* 31, no. 1 (2012): 87–96, https://psycnet.apa.org/record/2011-17888-001.

4. James Baraz and Shoshana Alexander, "The Helper's High," Greater Good Science Center, February 1, 2010, https://greatergood.berkeley.edu/article/item/the_helpers_high.

5. "Top 10 Facts That Make Redwood Trees Magnificent," Sempervirens Fund, accessed January 22, 2025, https://sempervirens.org/learn/redwood-facts/#fact-list.

6. *Our Epidemic of Loneliness and Isolation: The U.S. Surgeon General's Advisory on the Healing Effects of Social Connection and Community* (Office of the U.S. Surgeon General, 2023), www.hhs.gov/sites/default/files/surgeon-general-social-connection-advisory.pdf.

CHAPTER 10: PRAY BOLDLY

1. This quote from the Catholic Catechism is sometimes attributed to Saint Ignatius and other times to Saint Augustine. Trent Horn, "St. Ignatius Said What?," Catholic Answers, July 31, 2019, www.catholic.com/magazine/online-edition/st-ignatius-said-what.

2. Though some have attributed this quote to Abraham Lincoln, research shows that the earliest rendition was ascribed to an anonymous lumberjack. "Quote Origin: To Cut Down a Tree in Five Minutes Spend Three Minutes Sharpening Your Axe," Quote Investigator, March 29, 2014, https://quoteinvestigator.com/2014/03/29/sharp-axe/.

3. This is a footnote of Matthew 6:13, NIV.

CHAPTER 11: PREPARE FOR SETBACKS

1. C. S. Lewis, *The Problem of Pain* (Macmillan, 1962), 93.
2. Greg Lukianoff and Jonathan Haidt, *The Coddling of the American Mind: How Good Intentions and Bad Ideas Are Setting Up a Generation for Failure* (Penguin, 2018), 22.

CONCLUSION

1. Oliver Burkeman, *Four Thousand Weeks: Time Management for Mortals* (Farrar, Straus and Giroux, 2021), 198.

About the Author

RUSLAN KD is a Christian YouTuber, podcaster, and entrepreneur known for his thought-provoking commentary on faith, culture, and personal development. Originally an Armenian refugee from Baku, Azerbaijan, he immigrated to the U.S. as a child. A former independent artist, Ruslan transitioned to digital media, where he creates content that bridges biblical wisdom with real-world issues. Through his YouTube channels, Ruslan KD and Bless God Studios, he explores topics such as apologetics, cultural trends, and practical stewardship, inspiring audiences to live with purpose and intentionality. In addition to his online presence, he is a sought-after speaker and lives in California with his wife and children.

Author social media: @RuslanKD